The Blueprint

To order additional copies of *The Blueprint,* by Rico Hill and Jared Thurmon,
call 1-800-765-6955.
Visit us at **www.reviewandherald.com** for information
on other Review and Herald® products.

The Blueprint

A MANUAL FOR REACHING THE CITIES

RICO HILL | JARED THURMON

REVIEW AND HERALD® PUBLISHING ASSOCIATION
Since 1861 | www.reviewandherald.com

Review and Herald® titles may be purchased in bulk for educational, business, fund-raising, or sales promotional use. For information, e-mail SpecialMarkets@reviewandherald.com.

The Review and Herald® Publishing Association publishes biblically based materials for spiritual, physical, and mental growth and Christian discipleship.

Texts credited to ARV are from *The Holy Bible,* edited by the American Revision Committee, Thomas Nelson & Sons, 1901.

Texts credited to ASV are from *The Holy Bible,* edited by the American Revision Committee, Standard Edition, Thomas Nelson & Sons, 1901.

Scripture quotations marked NASB are from the *New American Standard Bible,* copyright © 1960, 1962, 1963, 1968, 1971, 1972, 1973, 1975, 1977, 1995 by The Lockman Foundation Used by permission.

This book was
Edited by Gerald Wheeler
Copyedited by Delma Miller
Interior designed by Johanna Wolfe
Cover design by Emily Ford / Review and Herald® Design Center
Typeset: Minion Pro 13/15

PRINTED IN U.S.A.

17 16 15 14 13   5 4 3 2 1

Library of Congress Cataloging-in-Publication Data

Hill, Rico.
  The blueprint : a manual for reaching the cities / Rico Hill and Jared Thurmon.
      pages cm
1. Church growth—Seventh-Day Adventists. 2. Church growth—North America. 3. City missions—North America. 4. Seventh-Day Adventists—North America—Membership. 5. Church membership—North America. I. Title.
  BV652.25.H55 2013

266'.6732—dc23   2012051436

  ISBN 978-0-8280-2714-4

DEDICATION

This book is first and foremost dedicated to Jesus Christ and the resurrection of His method of reaching people for the kingdom as demonstrated in the Synoptic Gospels, modeled by the New Testament believers, and revealed for His end-time people very specifically in Isaiah 58 and Matthew 25. Christ mingled or "integrated" Himself into every aspect of the lives of the people as He demonstrated the method of reaching the cities of His day. He was the epitome of personal evangelism, the quintessential relational evangelist.

"Jesus saw in every soul one to whom must be given the call to His kingdom. He reached the hearts of the people by going among them as one who desired their good. He sought them in the public streets, in private houses, on the boats, in the synagogue, by the shores of the lake, and at the marriage feast. He met them at their daily vocations, and manifested an interest in their secular affairs. He carried His instruction into the household, bringing families in their own homes under the influence of His divine presence. His strong, personal sympathy helped to win hearts" (*The Desire of Ages,* p. 151).

It is also dedicated to our families who have supported our efforts, our Beehive board of directors who continue to offer wisdom, prayers, and godly counsel, and the many dedicated men and women who have been inspirational in introducing this ministry and then have stood by and helped it grow.

Finally, *The Blueprint* is dedicated to those who are committed to the mission of the church, seeking to engage, equip, and empower members, small groups, and ministries, and to unite their efforts for the gospel commission under the principles modeled in Scripture and reinforced by the writings of Ellen G. White. It is dedicated to those who long to see revival and reformation *now* and try earnestly to demonstrate the gospel in every possible way as a witness so that the end can come.

—RICO HILL AND JARED THURMON

CONTENTS

PREFACE

Below are some statistical data and trends of Adventism in North America. We realize that it is just one of the church's world divisions, but it seems to share some common characteristics with other divisions in the developed world.

1. In the past 30 years the number of members needed to produce one baptism has almost doubled, from 15 to nearly 30. In addition, we now spend up to about $41,000 per conversion, up from about $5,500 (2005 U.S. dollars) in 1913.[1]

2. In order to exceed the population growth rate and thus experience meaningful increase, the church must expand beyond the 2 percent level. In the past 100 years we have exceeded the 5 percent growth level only twice. The first time was during the First World War in 1917, the second time during the Great Depression in 1935.[2]

3. North American population rose by 1.31 percent yearly from 1913 till 1975, but the church grew by 3.61 percent. However, from 1975 to 2005 North American expansion slowed to 1.09 percent yearly, while the church dropped to 0.06 percent. This indicates that the Seventh-day Adventist presence is shrinking in the North American Division.[3]

4. New membership in the NAD comes mainly from the African descent demographic. This group makes up approximately 30 percent of the NAD membership, compared to its 12.8 percent share of the population. *Though we rejoice in the diversity of the church, this figure shows that NAD is not effectively reaching the Caucasian descent group.*[4]

5. In 2008 *the median age of Adventists in the NAD was 51 years, while the median age in the population was 36.* Such numbers mean the church is not doing well in keeping or attracting young believers. The church seems to be surviving by the energy and resources of previous generations. But if this graying trend continues, what is going to happen when those supportive generations fade into the sunset?[5]

6. Cultural shifts that attach more authority to personal experience and more distrust to institutions are making people less interested in church, though interest in spiritual things remains strong.[6]

7. According to an August 1, 2010, article in the New York *Times*, pastors are experiencing a decline in personal health as well as family happiness. Perhaps a large part of this results from church members delegating too many responsibilities onto the pastor.[7]

For the preceding reasons and others not mentioned, we believe the time has come to address the cause of such issues. God has told us that the greatest moments of the church's history still lie before us. If that is true, then we must do something to reverse those trends that say otherwise.

We believe the secret rests in the following pages.

---

[1] www.ministrymagazine.org/archive/2010/december/reflections-on-the-future-of-north-american-seventh-day-adventism.html.

[2] All the statistics related to the Seventh-day Adventist Church come from the Office of Archives, Statistics, and Research of the North American Division, www.adventistarchives.org/documents.asp?CatID=27&SortBy=1& ShowDateOrder=True (May 2008).

[3] *Ibid.*

[4] The population figure came from www.census.gov/and http://eh.net. In 1913, 97 million people lived in the United States and 8 million in Canada, totaling 105 million for the NAD. In 2005 the United States had a population of 298 million and Canada had 32 million, totaling 330 million for the NAD.

[5] Monte Sahlin, *Adventist Congregations Today* (Lincoln, Nebr.: Center for Creative Ministry, 2003), pp. 35, 36. See also Monte Sahlin and Paul Richardson, *Seventh-day Adventists in North America: A Demographic Profile* (Milton-Freewater, Oreg.: Center for Creative Ministry, 2008), pp. 5, 6.

[6] Statistics of the North American Division, www.adventistarchives.org/documents.asp?CatID=27&SortBy=1& ShowDateOrder=True (May 2008).

[7] www.nytimes.com/2010/08/02/nyregion/02burnout.html?pagewanted=all; https://www.ministrymagazine.org/archive/2011/02/the-long-view-of-church-growth.html.

INTRODUCTION

Statistics show that our beloved church is aging, is not keeping up with population growth rates, is spending more to win fewer converts, and, for all intents and purposes, has abandoned the kind of evangelism that produces disciples after the Acts model. We are seeing some disturbing trends that will in a few short years render the church irrelevant. Can we afford to sit idly by and watch, anticipating the huge 40 percent drop that will surely come when many of the faithful pass on? We are going down the wrong road. The farther we travel it, the longer it will take to get back to the right road. We can either keep heading in the same direction or turn around and prepare for the inevitable. By being strategic, we can reverse the trends.

When the Lord impressed upon this ministry to write a book regarding the Beehive concept as a blueprint to reach the cities, we initially understood that it would be one that individuals could read and gain some insight about how the ministry providentially began. However, when the word "manual" was introduced into the title, we reflected on what purpose or purposes a manual actually serves. When someone purchases a car, it always comes with a manual. It outlines every aspect of that car and how it functions: what type of gas gives it optimal performance; what type of battery is most effective in running the electrical system; and even down to the ideal tire pressure that will guarantee safety and good gas mileage on long journeys. Therefore, a car owner's manual is more than just a book. It is something you always keep in your car for quick reference. Even after those exciting hours of reading about your new car and all the wonderful things it can do, the manual is always something that you keep available, as it will help you operate your car at maximum efficiency. And should you sell or pass on the vehicle to someone else, the manual goes with the vehicle. Why? So that the new owner will also know exactly how to maintain the vehicle in good condition. And so it is with this manual.

As God's remnant church we have an incredible responsibility. The very word "remnant" has such explicit connotations that we cannot escape the very responsibilities placed on us as a people. In fact, we proudly wear the name as a badge of honor and hold it up as a distinction in our evangelistic efforts. But evangelistically we need to reconsider what we are saying to the world and ourselves when we do so. When we explain the word "remnant," drawing an analogy to a remnant sale of leftover fabric from the original bolt, we should give solemn consideration to the very analogy itself. In the context of our outreach efforts and methodology, think about what the remnant fabric cannot be. It cannot be a different pattern or material than the original. Thus it cannot be stripes when the original was checkered, have a different texture, or be cotton when the original was leather. Now think about what characteristics the remnant must have. Put simply, it must have the same colors, patterns, stitching, etc. Whatever methods we as the remnant church might employ to reach the cities, they must match those of the original.

Further, making use of that remnant fabric imagery, we can create pants, shirts, skirts, dresses, or caps, but they must all have the characteristics of the original pattern. This is the position of the Beehive manual. It is not only a call to get back to the original methodology, but to use those approaches in the most creative and innovative ways that will keep up with our ever-shifting world. While we acknowledge that some of our efforts have resulted from much creative thinking, however, when it abandons the original pattern, it excludes the Great Originator and leads to confusion, internal strife, and failure. The time has come to get back to Bible-inspired principles, using the best ideas while abandoning methods made popular by those in Christendom who have never discerned the pattern but instead rely more on convenient cultural trends, human wisdom, and tradition.

We pray this Beehive manual will galvanize the remnant church to do some critical thinking as we seek to reach this final generation. Not a book to read and then place on a bookshelf, it should be used as a guide to keep the church running at its Holy Spirit-powered capacity. Nothing short of strict, implicit adherence to the instructions given by God in His Word and through His prophet will shore up His remnant church for this final leg on our long journey home. By God's grace, this manual seeks to outline, in a practical way, how God's church can reach the cities and finish His mission on earth: Christ as the driver and fueled only by His Holy Spirit.

"Christ's method alone will give true success in reaching the people. The Saviour mingled with men as one who desired their good. He showed His sympathy for them, ministered to their needs, and won their confidence. Then He bade them, 'Follow Me'" (*The Ministry of Healing*, p. 143).

"It is the privilege of every Christian not only to look for but to hasten the coming of our Lord Jesus Christ (2 Peter 3:12, margin). Were all who profess His name bearing fruit to His glory, how quickly the whole world would be sown with the seed of the gospel. Quickly the last great harvest would be ripened, and Christ would come to gather the precious grain" (*Christ's Object Lessons,* p. 69).

"By giving the gospel to the world it is in our power to hasten our Lord's return. We are not only to look for but to hasten the coming of the day of God" (*The Desire of Ages,* p. 633).

"He has put it in our power, through cooperation with Him, to bring this scene of misery to an end" (*Education,* p. 264).

CHAPTER 1

HOW TO USE THIS MANUAL

The objective of *The Blueprint* is to bring out biblical principles that inspire, equip, and empower church members to engage in God's final mission so that Jesus will come and take us home. Our prayer is that God's methods from the Bible, the apostolic example, and the counsel of the writings of Ellen G. White will inspire every church, no matter where they are. It is time for the final push, and the church must bring to bear all of its gifts, talents, ministries, and means for God's use. Now is not the time to store up treasures on earth. All that we have must be given to the work, as treasures deposited in heaven.

We should note that while this ministry has not attained every aspect, as outlined in Ellen White's dream seen in the next chapter, it is the goal and should be the goal of every congregation or group someday to have all facets or components working at the same time. The wisdom that you will find in these pages is how God has led us step by step according to the blueprint, advancing a phase at a time as the Lord leads. Never should we be discouraged if it cannot all happen at once, nor should we be overconfident if money is no object and it can happen quickly. Although He could have, Christ did not come as a mature, adult man. Instead, God's plan for success started at the beginning, compromising not even the slightest detail. The writers of this manual have learned much as they laid the foundation of this concept in two cities, and feel that they can offer the wisdom needed to get started. God has shown that to sit and wait and do nothing is unacceptable. Remember, "even God . . . calleth those things which be not as though they were" (Rom. 4:17). Initiating the Beehive method in all of its forms is a faith venture and requires a trust in God every step of the way. When getting started, a church or group must decide that it will endeavor to create the entire Beehive, either through its own resources or through partnerships with others. So no matter where you start, commence with that which lies closest at hand.

Who Should Read This Beehive Manual?

They include those looking for something to get the church motivated and back on track but just don't know where to start, as well as small groups that feel impressed to get more involved in the church's mission, but are discouraged because it seems as though no one else senses the urgency. Church ministries that have been languishing will also want to embrace it. We recommend that while the use of the Beehive manual can start with individuals, they should gather others to go through it together. Groups offer the best opportunity for brainstorming and breakout sessions in which ideas can find a sounding board and each of its members can be strengthened as they work within the dynamics of group interaction.

Therefore the Beehive manual has laid out succinctly, but comprehensively, how to get going and maintain momentum, for Christ has said to go quickly into all the world—the streets and lanes of the cities, the highways and the hedges—and compel them to come so that His house may be full. And if your church is not full, something is wrong and you are in need of this manual. Are you ready to go? Then here's the first thing you need to do to get started.

Pray

First of all, *pray, pray, pray.* Prayer is the answer to every problem in life. It puts us in tune with divine wisdom, and divine wisdom knows how to adjust everything perfectly.

Often we do not pray in certain situations, because, from our standpoint, the outlook is hopeless. But nothing is impossible with God. Nothing is so entangled that He cannot remedy it. No human relationship is too strained that God cannot bring about reconciliation and understanding. No habit is so deep-rooted that it cannot be overcome. No one is so weak that he or she cannot be healed. And no mind is so dull that it cannot be made brilliant.

Whatever we need, if we trust God, He will supply it. If anything is causing worry and anxiety, let us stop rehearsing the difficulty and trust God for healing, love, and power.

"Be careful for nothing; but in every thing by prayer and supplication with thanksgiving let your requests be made known unto God" (Phil. 4:6).

Before continuing a page or even a word further, stop and pray that God will accomplish in you personally what He intends through this Beehive manual. Pray that your thoughts, your will, your attitude, and your attention would come under the lordship of Jesus Christ. If you are a part of a group, pray that each member of it would take hold of the mission outlined herein with the Spirit of Christ. In fact, as a group it would be helpful to read the *40 Days* books, by Dennis Smith. Use these books and begin to pray for the outpouring of God's Holy Spirit over the reading and studying of this manual, your group, and your church. Ask the Father to search the inner chambers of your heart and help you identify the defects and the selfish motives in your character that will hinder you from moving forward with the principles outlined in this manual. Second, ask God to show you how those defects will hinder, injure, delay, or in any way short-circuit what He ignited long ago when He gave the Holy Ghost to His church. Then pray that by His wonderful, amazing grace He will enable you to surrender each and every defect and selfish motivation so that He may reign supreme and bless His work. Pray that He will consecrate you for His service. Pray that He will cover you, your group, your ministry, and your church with the full armor of God. Then, as a group, or family, pray for your church and its leadership. While it may seem excessive, it is absolutely necessary. There are reasons that our world, our homes, and even our beloved church are struggling. We are caught in a great conflict between good and evil, and prayer casts our vote on the winning team. But we must pray for the strength that will be necessary, as our adversary is already standing poised to destroy our efforts, and he has enlisted agencies all around us to stop our work in its tracks. Consider Dennis Smith's *40 Days* books on prayer. Whatever you do, begin the process with prayer.

Pray. Exalt God's Word. The Bible is called the Word of God for a reason. It is His book of promise. The greatest promise was that His Word would be made flesh and would dwell among us. It was His promise in the beginning, and He fulfilled it in Christ. Grab hold of your favorite promise or axiom and make it your battle cry. The apostle Paul said:

"I can do all things through Christ which strengtheneth me" (Phil. 4:13).

"But my God shall supply all your needs according to his riches in glory by Christ Jesus" (verse 19).

"For I determined not to know any thing among you, save Jesus Christ, and him crucified" (1 Cor. 2:2).

"I am crucified with Christ: nevertheless I live; yet not I, but Christ liveth in me: and the life which I now live in the flesh I live by the faith of the Son of God, who loved me, and gave himself for me" (Gal. 2:20).

John said in his First Epistle: "And this is the confidence that we have in him, that, if we ask any thing according to his will, he heareth us: And if we know that he hear us, whatsoever we ask, we know that we have the petitions that we desired of him" (1 John 5:14, 15).

Feel free to use your favorite promises, "for all the promises of God in him are yea, and in him Amen, unto the glory of God by us" (2 Cor. 1:20). Determine, by God's grace and the power of His Word, that you will not be shaken when you begin to move as God directs.

Discuss

Now whether you have done this preparatory work as an individual or as a group, it is time to go prayerfully through the chapters of the Beehive manual. Each chapter ends with a set of questions for discussion. This is absolutely necessary. Discussion will help bring the group together. It will assist in deepening the impression, as the ideas communicated are digested, repeated, and articulated by each member of the group. The intent is to explore within your group the particulars of the chapter—to reflect on where your church is in light of what you have learned. But the discussion must begin with prayer. Carefully and honestly examine the strengths and weaknesses of your particular congregation. Long discourses about what's going on at the church across town or the world church will not be helpful. It is your church that you should evaluate. What isn't working is as much a reflection of you as anything else. Conversely, what is working will also reveal what you are contributing to your congregation. The tone is not to be critical, but constructive, with a genuine desire to foster unity and implement solid plans to move the church forward. Always remember the objective (to reach the cities and prepare a people for the coming of the Lord) and stay on track.

As you discuss issues, have a dry-erase board or a flipchart handy to jot down thoughts and ideas that you can expand upon as you seek to implement a working program for your congregation. Remember, find every excuse to pause and pray as your discussions progress through the chapters. If an idea is so amazing that everyone cheers, stop, pray, and give honor and glory to God. It all belongs to Him. He is the captain of the ship. Every good gift comes from Him. As you keep Him in the midst of this work, taking no credit but leaning on Him and thanking and glorifying Him, your discussions will be fruitful.

"Christ's workers are to obey His instructions implicitly. The work is God's, and if we would bless others His plans must be followed. Self cannot be made a center; self can receive no honor. If we plan according to our own ideas, the Lord will leave us to our own mistakes. But when, after following His directions, we are brought into strait places, He will deliver us. . . . Often we shall be surrounded with trying circumstances, and then, in the fullest confidence, we must depend upon God" (*The Desire of Ages,* p. 369).

CHAPTER 2

BLUEPRINT IN THE BAY AREA

To understand better how to reach the cities and how we can get closer to the people through integrated personal evangelism, we need to first see the beauty of the blueprint given to Ellen G. White in a dream that met its fulfillment in the San Francisco Bay Area in 1901.

While the writers of this Beehive manual would love to take credit for something so clever, so innovative and seamless, they cannot. Ellen White received this amazing concept of how to finish God's work on earth in a cryptic dream about a beehive. We present it just as she penned it in the Australasian *Union Conference Record*, March 1, 1901.

"It would be difficult to describe my feelings as I stood before the San Francisco church, Sabbath, November 10, and looked over the large congregation. My mind went back to the time, twenty-four years ago, when my husband and I were planning for the building of a house of worship in San Francisco. Some, when they saw the plan, said, 'It is too large. The house will never be filled.' At the same time we were erecting the first building of the Pacific Press and the meeting-house in Oakland. How great was the anxiety felt, and how earnest the prayers offered to God that He would open the way for the advancement of these enterprises!

"At that time I dreamed that I saw two bee hives, one in San Francisco and one in Oakland. In the hive in Oakland the bees were diligently at work. Then I looked at the hive in San Francisco, and saw very little being done. The hive in Oakland seemed to be far the more promising. After a time my attention was again called to the hive in San Francisco, and I saw that an entire change had taken place. Great activity was seen among the bees. <u>They were earnestly at work.</u>

"When I related this dream, it was interpreted to mean that in San Francisco there was a great work to be done. There were among us at that time only a few men to whom we could look for large financial assistance. Believers were few in number, and we needed much courage and much faith to brace us for work.

"We prayed much in regard to the necessities of the cause and the meaning of the dream, and resolved to venture out in accordance with the light given. My husband and I decided to sell our property in Battle Creek, that we might use the proceeds in this work. We wrote to our brethren, 'Sell everything we have in Battle Creek, and send us the money at once.' This was done, and we helped to build the churches in Oakland and San Francisco. And the Lord revealed to us that although at first the work in San Francisco would move slowly, yet it would make steady advancement, and San Francisco would become a great center. The Lord would inspire men by His Holy Spirit to carry forward the work with faith and courage and perseverance.

"Before leaving Australia, I dreamed that I was standing before a large congregation in San Francisco; that the Lord gave me a message to bear, and freedom in bearing this message. The people had ears to hear, and hearts to understand. When we entered the San Francisco church Sabbath morning we found it crowded to its utmost capacity. As I stood before the people, I thought of the dream and the instruction which had been given me so many years ago, and I was much encouraged. Looking at the people assembled, I felt that I could indeed say, The Lord has fulfilled His word. After I had finished speaking, all who wished to give themselves to the Lord in solemn consecration were invited to come forward. To this invitation two hundred persons responded. This was a time of precious refreshing. We knew the angels of God were with us. The room was pervaded with the atmosphere of heaven.

"Among those who came forward were some who were entering the Lord's service for the first time, and some who had been attending our meetings and had become interested in the Advent message. May they decide to place themselves wholly on the Lord's side. May they have the courage to receive and live the truth. I felt from my heart that we could say to them, 'Come thou with us, and we will do thee good; for the Lord hath spoken good concerning Israel. . . . It shall be if thou go with us, yea, it shall be, that what goodness the Lord shall do unto us, the same will we do unto thee.'

"We were much pleased by the spirit shown by those assembled. They freely acknowledged the goodness and mercy of God, offering Him praise and thanksgiving. The Lord is glorified when His people praise Him.

"At the close of the meeting many pressed forward to take my hand and welcome me back to America. I was very glad to meet them. From Elder J. O. Corliss, who is pastor of the San Francisco church, we learn that there are many lines of Christian effort being carried forward by our brethren and sisters in San Francisco. These include visiting the sick and destitute, finding homes for orphans, and work for the unemployed; nursing the sick, and teaching the love of Christ from house to house; the distribution of literature; and the conducting of classes for healthful living and the care of the sick. A school for the children is conducted in the basement of the meeting-house. In another part of the city a workingmen's home and medical mission is maintained. On Market Street, near the City Hall, there is a bath establishment, operated as a branch of the St. Helena Sanitarium. In the same locality is a depot of the Health Food Company, where health foods are not only sold, but instruction is given as to reforms in diet.

"Nearer the center of the city, our people conduct a Vegetarian Cafe, which is open six days in the week, and is entirely closed on the Sabbath. Here about five hundred meals are served daily, and no flesh-meats are used.

"Dr. and Mrs. Dr. Lamb are doing much medical work for the poor in connection with their regular practice; and Dr. Buchannan is doing much free work at the Workingmen's Home. At the Medical and Dental schools in the city, there are about 20 of our young people in attendance.

"We earnestly hope that the steps taken in the future in the work in San Francisco will still be steps of progress. The work that has been done there is but a beginning. San Francisco is a world in itself, and the Lord's work there is to broaden and deepen. Souls are to be sought for. The word of the Lord is to be declared, line upon line, precept upon precept, that His name may be glorified.

"God will use consecrated ability in His service. As His servants impart to others that which they receive, He will entrust them with more to impart. And as they are enabled through His grace to accomplish good, they will ascribe all the glory to Him who is the Alpha and the Omega, the first and the last. Thus divinity and humanity work together. Men become laborers together with God, working out their own salvation with fear and trembling, realizing always that it is God who works in them to will and to do of His good pleasure.

"There is a great work to be done in San Francisco and Oakland. The Lord will use humble men in these great cities. He can work with those who will labor in His fear. He will give evidence of His power to sincere workers and to sincere inquirers after truth, those who desire not only to know but also to do His will.

"There are men and women whom the Lord, through peculiar circumstances, will bring to the front in His work. These will be men and women who have consecrated themselves to Him. As they walk before Him in faith and trust, He will lead them to places of usefulness and honor. To those who rely upon Him He is a present help in every time of need. Those who honor His name He will qualify for important and perilous service. They may not have time to obtain all the education they desire, but the great Teacher understands. What He calls for is the willing devotion of heart and mind. When this is given Him, He will fit the givers for His service, in spite of apparent difficulties and obstacles. In His name and in His strength they will go forth to conquer.

"God is testing the motives and principles of men and women. Strong faith and much prayer will bring heavenly angels to our side. By patient continuance in well-doing, we become channels of light.

"Those who are willing to be emptied of self will be fitted for the Lord's work. There is work for all who will deny self and lift the cross. Through the help of the Holy Spirit they will gain the victories, which God desires them to gain. Wisdom and strength will reward energy and perseverance. These are God's gifts to the diligent, humble worker."

What Do We Take From This Now and How Do We Apply It?

Make no mistake about it, those active in both San Francisco and Oakland during the turn of the century were busy (like a beehive), because they saw what they did as an end-time work. Ellen White constantly admonished the church to evangelize the cities before it was too late.

A Few Key Points to the Vision

1. The Beehive dream fulfillment began with a mission-minded congregation that was to be the core element of "centers of influence."

Church members were involved in many kinds of activity. The love and work of the church spilled out into the city streets, and the community became a mission field. In other words, the church had become relevant in that society as it integrated itself into various aspects of life.

2. Much prayer and faith were critical at every step to accomplish the necessities of the dream.

3. In accordance with the light given, church members resolved to venture out.

4. Leading by example, Ellen and James White and some in Battle Creek were willing to "sell everything" and use the proceeds for God's work. "This was done."

5. Her dream and its interpretation were sure, so that Ellen White could say, "The Lord has fulfilled His word."

6. The Lord revealed that San Francisco would be a "great center."

It suggests that there would be others, but San Francisco would be a hub, so to speak. God had intended that what happened there would spread outward, beyond the Bay Area.

7. The church reaped a harvest and experienced revival. As a result of their faithfulness, "two hundred persons" responded and "this was a time of precious refreshing."

Is it possible that by the time Ellen White spoke at San Francisco that those 200 people had experienced the love of members of this congregation through the Beehive concept while they were still outside of the church?

8. At the close of the meetings Ellen and James discovered that there were "many lines of Christian effort being carried forward." They constituted a complete and comprehensive "city mission" that consisted of such projects as:

a. visiting the sick and destitute (health-related)

b. aiding widows and orphans

c. operating a workingmen's home and finding work for the unemployed

d. nursing the sick (health-related)

e. teaching the love of Christ from house to house

f. literature distribution

g. healthful living classes and the care of the sick (health-related)

h. an Adventist school for children

i. a medical mission at the homeless shelter (health-related)

j. a health food store that gave nutritional and other instruction (health-related)

k. a bath/hygiene establishment (health-related)

l. an outpost or lifestyle center of St. Helena Sanitarium (health-related)

m. a vegetarian café on Market Street (health-related)

n. doctors who volunteered their time (along with medical and dental students) to serve the poor (health-related)

Such "lines of effort" or "centers of influence" made up the beehive that Ellen White saw in her dream. We believe that this was and is the prototype for our city missions today. Note that of the 14 categories of activity listed, more than half (nine) touch upon areas of health. We believe that such an emphasis offered further assurance that the program was from God, established by His divine providence, as it calls our attention back to Christ, the Great Physician, who did more healing than preaching. And since Christ is our great medical missionary, wouldn't He inspire His closing work to have healing prominently at its center?

We believe that because of the neglect of this work in the early part of the twentieth century, another aspect has been added to what Ellen White witnessed. As always, we turn to the Bible for the principle.

First we find it in the parable of the sheep and goats in Matthew 25. In it Christ points out several things that were done or not done as He separates the two classes: "Inasmuch as ye have done it unto one of the least of these my brethren, ye have done it unto me" (verse 40).

That which someone did for Christ or the least and that which a person did not do for Christ or the least are one and the same. Notice who the "least" are in verses 35, 36: "For I was an hungred, and ye gave me meat: I was thirsty, and ye gave me drink: I was a stranger, and ye took me in: naked, and ye clothed me: I was sick, and ye visited me: I was in prison, and ye came unto me." Notice the various categories:

a. the hungry
b. the thirsty
c. the stranger
d. the naked
e. the sick
f. the prisoner

First of all, this shows us where we are in the closing moments. It is not a coincidence that, while each category is important to Christ, the last two are "the sick" and "the prisoner." It is our belief that, based on the Holy Bible, ministering to the sick and those in prison should form a significant part of the last great evangelistic push before Jesus comes. Notice further the last two acts that Jesus performs just before His death on the cross. They involved healing and "prison ministry."

"And one of them smote the servant of the high priest, and cut off his right ear. And Jesus answered and said, Suffer ye thus far. And he touched his ear, and healed him" (Luke 22:50, 51).

The next-to-the-last great act that Jesus performs is His restoration of Malchus' ear when Peter slices it off. Now here is the final thing He does before He finishes the work of redemption: "There they crucified him, and the malefactors, one on the right hand, and the other on the left" (Luke 23:33). "And he said unto Jesus, Lord, remember me when thou comest into thy kingdom. And Jesus said unto him, Verily I say unto thee, To day shalt thou be with me in paradise" (verses 42, 43). He demonstrated His concern for a prisoner.

If it is hard to believe that this was important to Christ or that it is indeed a demonstration of what God's remnant people will do, we need look no further than the book of Hebrews for the principle: "Remember them that are in bonds, as bound with them; and them which suffer adversity, as being yourselves also in the body" (Heb. 13:3).

Scripture records that one of Christ's last acts of love before He completed the work of redemption was to heal a man and pardon a genuinely guilty prisoner. For this reason we believe that similar things will be part of what God will do in the last days through His remnant people. So we have added prison ministry to the 14 areas of integrated evangelism seen in the Beehive structure.

DISCUSSION BREAKOUT SESSION WORKSHEET

Assignment 1

As a group, discuss in detail the Beehive dream as outlined in the previous chapter. Consider why God gave so little specific information, but cloaked the dream in the imagery of a beehive.

In a beehive, they were earnestly at work

Assignment 2

Before Ellen White even understood the Beehive dream, she and her husband took several bold steps. Describe some of the characteristics of their actions that led to what happened in San Francisco.

to sell there property in Battle Creek, to build a church in Oakland and San Francisco

Assignment 3

Discuss the "Christian efforts" referred to in the description given by Ellen White. Are they outdated? If so, how can we apply them in principle in our day?

No

Assignment 4

As a group, discuss the term *centers of influence*. Is your church a source of influence in your community, your town or city? If yes, discuss how. If not, explore why that is not the case.

Assignment 5

Consider how your church can expand beyond its walls and become the nucleus for a center of influence or beehive.

Assignment 6

Discuss the term *integrated evangelism*. How can your congregation employ it in relationship to a prison, college campus, or homeless shelter?

get involed, but first we need to work together as a body.

CHAPTER 3

CHRIST'S METHOD: THE PERFECT BLUEPRINT

O n page 17 of *The Ministry of Healing* Ellen White describes Christ as coming "to this world as the unwearied servant of man's necessity." When God wanted to reach the cities of the world during the time of Christ, He sent His Son as the unsurpassed and epitomizing gesture of love and the supremely personal touch. Stated simply, a personal God showed up in person and pointedly declared, "When you have seen Me, you have seen the Father" (see John 14:9). The power of the Godhead could have sent Christ as a mature man, but no, He came as a zygote. He could have arrived at the very least as a teenager to minimize the risk, but no, He allowed Himself to develop as a fetus and then be born in a manger. What amazing condescension! If He was going to be a servant of humanity's necessity, it was critical that He pass through every experience that a human being could possibly have. In other words, Christ was following a blueprint that we see prophesied in part in Psalm 139:15, 16: "My substance was not hid from thee, when I was made in secret, and curiously wrought in the lowest parts of the earth. Thine eyes did see my substance, yet being unperfect [embryonic]; and in thy book all my members were written, which in continuance were fashioned, when as yet there was none of them."

Anyone who builds something—whether it's an electronic device, a home, or a kingdom—must begin with a blueprint if it is to be made correctly. The Sovereign One of heaven sees it no differently. Christ was to begin when a virgin would conceive of the Holy Ghost (Isa. 7:14). He was to advance step by step, according to a divine blueprint, as an embryo "fearfully and wonderfully made." The blueprint said that "a baby would be born in a manger," and not one step was skipped. You see that Christ, following the blueprint, would have to flee the dangerous city of Nazareth and grow up in Egypt in an environment conducive for the Son of God to develop in "wisdom and stature, and in favour with God and man" (Luke 2:52). A God with infinite wisdom and unmatched power prepared a plan and followed it perfectly.

As if that were not enough, a perfectly set prophetic clock reinforced the divine blueprint's accuracy: "When the fulness of the time was come, God sent forth his Son, made of a woman, made under the law" (Gal. 4:4). Christ even left the carpentry shop and began His ministry on time and according to the blueprint. If we could break down the order of how He set up His ministry to its simplest level, it would go something like this:

1. Christ starts a church of 12 men (Matt. 10:1, 2).
2. By example, He begins to train them to cast out demons and heal disease.
3. The church grows to 82, after 70 more are added (Luke 10:1).

4. They all experience on-the-job training, beginning right where they were.
5. Those added included women whom Jesus healed (Luke 8:2).
6. Several of the women who had been healed now ministered to Him from their own money/substance (verse 3).
7. As a result of all that had happened so far, "much people were gathered together, and were come to him out of every city" (verse 4).

If we are going to reach the cities, we must follow the blueprint established by the Master. We cannot improve upon the methods of Christ. What He accomplished inspiration then caused to be written down for our learning and for us to follow. By way of principle Solomon stated that "the thing that hath been, it is that which shall be; and that which is done is that which shall be done: and there is no new thing under the sun. Is there any thing whereof it may be said, See, this is new? it hath been already of old time, which was before us" (Eccl. 1:9, 10).

Indeed, there is nothing that is new under the sun. We can attempt new methods, but "except the Lord build the house, they labour in vain that build it" (Ps. 127:1). And if the Lord is the builder of ministry on this earth, then it safe to say that He followed His own blueprint. So the best we can do is to employ His plans. But the Lord will allow us to use new brushes and add a new coat of paint.

Daniel 12:4 tells us that just before Jesus returns "knowledge shall be increased." Many have interpreted it as the spread of science and technology. And we have certainly witnessed that. As soon as you think you have the latest and coolest cell phone, Blackberry, iPhone, or iPad, a month later newer and more technologically superior devices enter the market, making yours ridiculously out-of-date.

But we could also see in the passage spiritual advances relative to innovation in witnessing and spreading the gospel. In other words, the method remains the same, but the knowledge increases of how best to implement the blueprint in a constantly changing world. We can see how Bible knowledge increased in the case of the books of Daniel and Revelation. In the early 1800s our understanding of them made relatively gigantic leaps, comparable to that of the Industrial Revolution. It was an awakening of sorts. Application of that which was there all the time became "fresh and new." But it wasn't new at all. It had been there all the time. We just saw it in new ways. And we must continue that same kind of searching and reexamining of the old paths to see what we have missed. We should not slow down in our efforts to find new ways to employ God's methods to reach the lost, just as the world of technology never seems to stop in its search to invent the latest gadget and reach the masses.

Today, while we can peer into faraway galaxies with Hubble space technology and cars can parallel-park themselves, the innovation that goes into evangelism does not seem to be keeping the same pace, particularly in our efforts to reach urban areas. Yes, technological advances have helped our large evangelistic programs and seminars. Superb graphics have added to their quality and have brought many to Christ. But are we following all the biblical guidelines and utilizing all the resources set forth for us in our labor for Christ? The cities of our world have become the habitation of some of the worst evils. As time lingers, they grow more and more difficult to penetrate as secularism explodes at an alarming rate. Have we looked to devise innovative methods to give the last gospel warning to those living in these cities? Have we taken a fresh look at the blueprint of Christ and sought to make new application?

Have we as God's last-day remnant people stalled in our efforts to reach the vast urban areas, especially in North America? While we have seen pockets of success elsewhere in the world, by and large, though, we're just not attracting city people to Christ to the extent that God calls us to do in the final work. Evangelists and church members send out brochures and postcards in the hope that thousands will come to our churches or auditoriums and take a stand for baptism. We expect them to be swayed by a heartfelt sermon that crescendos to a solemn appeal. But many in the world view such things as just tactics to get tithe-paying members into the pews. And in many instances they are correct. However, inspiration even points out that this is not the only way.

"There is need of coming close to the people by personal effort. If less time were given to sermonizing, and more time were spent in personal ministry, greater results would be seen" (*The Ministry of Healing*, p. 143).

"Salt must be mingled with the substance to which it is added; it must penetrate and infuse in order to preserve. So it is through personal contact and association that men are reached by the saving power of the gospel. They are not saved in masses, but as individuals. Personal influence is a power. We must come close to those whom we desire to benefit" (*Thoughts From the Mount of Blessing*, p. 36).

No longer do we see baptisms happen in the numbers that we once witnessed. Some have even sought to attract people through various entertainments, including interpretive dance and miming. As a result, many have begun to wonder if this is all we've got. Or if it is all that God intended for His closing work.

By the moving of God's Holy Spirit, however, a few ministries in different parts of the country began to understand that God has more in store. In California, Kansas, Florida, and Georgia, a certain concept began to emerge out of the writings of Ellen G. White that seemed to have eluded many a reader for the past 100 years. It was not because people weren't reading. Rather, it was as if something had hidden those inspired lines in plain sight. Pastors and experts on her writings alike, when asked about it, were completely unaware of the "beehive" incident. What was so astounding about this is the fact that several like-minded individuals seemed to have stumbled on it about the same time, but in different places around the country. Once again, one's thoughts go to how the Holy Spirit is able to unlock ideas that literally lay in front of our eyes for years.

It all began for some with a perusal into the book *Welfare Ministry* and the dream by Ellen White we outlined in chapter 2. It is important to note that she did not understand the dream, nor was she later taken into vision to clarify it, and no subsequent dreams offered any explanation. The mysterious concept incubated for 24 years. It was as if God were allowing His church to catch up with it. Eventually we did.

So there it was: a new method of outreach that was as old as the Great Commission itself, but glimmering with a new coat of paint. It was progressive and enterprising, yet rooted and grounded in the very methods of Jesus Christ—integrated personal evangelism.

"Christ's method alone will give true success in reaching the people. The Saviour mingled with men as one who desired their good. He showed His sympathy for them, ministered to their needs, and won their confidence. Then He bade them, 'Follow me'" (*The Ministry of Healing,* p. 143).

What a wonderful Savior who "mingled with men." Somehow along the way we have lost Christ's method and now bid people to follow us before we even befriend them or minister to their needs.

Imagine the surprise when newly elected General Conference president Ted Wilson began to unfold the world church's agenda to reach the cities by using the Beehive concept. Those who had already stumbled on this method were absolutely elated. It was a confirmation on the highest level. At his ASI (Adventist-laymen's Services and Industries) talk with leadership and his Fall Council and NAD Health Summit sermons, Wilson delineated a comprehensive strategy to reach the cities and called for everyone, at every level, to join in for the finishing of the work. It became clear that the Lord was about to do something amazing.

The laws in Christ's day did not prohibit Him from walking into a merchant's shop and sharing the good news of the kingdom. But the laws in many states of our day do, however. We often see signs posted outside of businesses and gated residential communities announcing "no soliciting" or "no proselytizing." So how does one "mingle" when hostile signage and laws strongly discourage such practices? How do we meet the people where they are? The Beehive manual will show how we can still, to a much greater extent, move among people and share the love of Christ to them. Reaching those living in the cities in these final days is a personal work. It must be innovative and enterprising, yet simple, leaning and depending upon divine wisdom. It will be accomplished through the Beehive concept—blending evangelistic practices into the very fabric of everyday life so that we may get closer to people, love them, and show them Christ.

In these last days our efforts to reach the cities must be accompanied by the same compassion that Jesus exhibited. And finally, we must take it to where the people are, which is primarily in the large cities of the world. "Go out quickly into the streets and lanes of the city, and bring in hither the poor, . . . and the maimed, and the halt, and the blind" (Luke 14:21).

DISCUSSION BREAKOUT SESSION WORKSHEET

Assignment 1

On a separate sheet of paper, list at least five ways that God has led you, your family, or even your church in the past.

_____

_____

Assignment 2

With your group, share two of your experiences that mean the most to you.

_____

_____

Assignment 3

Pause as a group and offer the Lord thanks for His providential leading in your life personally, your family, and your church.

_____

_____

Assignment 4

As a group, using the many facets of the Beehive concept (programs for the homeless, prison ministry, etc.), identify what areas would work best in your town or city.

_Getting to know people_____

_____

Assignment 5

Discuss as a group what areas of the Beehive concept your church is currently engaged in. What functions well and why? What doesn't work? Why?

_____

_____

CHAPTER 4

A BRAND-NEW OLD IDEA

Some of the previously outlined 14 categories of activity that were taking place during the Beehive in San Francisco are now without question dated. At least four will be difficult for some to wrap their minds around. We will focus on those four to generate a more contemporary understanding. But we must reemphasize that such methods of integrated outreach are timeless, for they are based on divine principles. The names or terms may become archaic, but the need and the mission remain ever needed.

Admittedly, different nonprofit organizations, ministries, and churches carry out many forms of this type of work. Sadly, however, God's remnant church, the church with the last-day message for the cities, does very little in these areas. While the programs conducted by non-Adventist agencies help many, they do not present the three angels' messages. It is not our intent to overlook modern-day orphanages and foster care or even Big Brothers/Big Sisters programs. Nor can we discount the Salvation Army's service to the poor or the work of Goodwill and its job-training and job-search programs. Speaking of the Salvation Army, the prophet of the Lord said that they were doing a good work, but it was not the same as ours (*Welfare Ministry,* p. 251). But just because they are helping those who are poor does not mean that we should leave it entirely to them. We have a different objective.

Therefore, we need to reexamine those areas that the Seventh-day Adventist Church has somewhat forgotten or, because of the outdated nature of the terms, have relegated to our past. So our objective here is twofold. First, we'd like to share for consideration what such ministries could look like in a Beehive structure. And second, we desire to call Seventh-day Adventists back to city mission work by taking a fresh look at those seemingly archaic methods as we redefine them for the twenty-first century.

Homes for Orphans in the Twenty-first Century?

When we think of orphanages, most of us today regard them as something relegated to the underdeveloped countries of the world. And the Seventh-day Adventist Church has such programs in many such regions. But in reality these programs should be taking place in the large cities of the developed world as well.

James 1:27 tells us: "Pure religion and undefiled before God and the Father is this, To visit the fatherless and widows in their affliction, and to keep himself unspotted from the world."

We find the key to understanding what an orphanage should look like as part of a city mission program here in the book of James. The apostle gives a description of "pure religion" in its simplest terms. The verb he uses is so clear. We must "visit" them. *Strong's Concordance* defines the word "visit" beyond what we normally comprehend it to mean. Obviously, a home for the fatherless is ideal. But when there is no orphanage and only foster care or a single-mother environment, the Bible calls for us to care for young people in these categories. Notice how the theme of the Beehive will continue as a pattern through each aspect of ministry we will examine. Again and again we will find ourselves coming back to the idea that God's last work in the city is a closely personal one. Here He summons men and women to visit the fatherless. He wants men to provide a fatherly influence. While women have a vital role to play, in many cases such children are fatherless, and since the Lord calls men to be the priest of the home, when a father is absent spiritual leadership is also missing. We pray that many homes will open up for those children who have no parents at all. Also, we hope that some will be inspired to open Seventh-day Adventist-operated foster homes. But when that is not possible we must provide a structured way to minister to children and widows in our cities.

In addition to providing homes to care for true orphans and foster children, we should find ways to minister to children who have only one parent. Many of today's foster children, including those in single-parent homes, require the nurturing care of mothers. Thus we see the need for missionary mothers, as they were referred to during the early 1900s. Millions in the world's cities have lost a parent to disease or some other tragedy. We can integrate them into a church family who will love them and care for them. As we begin to explore the needs in our cities, we must see whether we should establish homes for children who have lost their parents or have been given up for adoption. One way that would be helpful in facilitating this is to do a community survey and determine how many single-parent homes there are.

A "Workingmen's Home"

A "workingmen's home" is basically a modern-day homeless shelter. But beyond that, it should be a place where those who are seeking to get back on their feet or perhaps are trying to make a change in life can find spiritual rest and education for a better life. Think of the many men and women with felonies on their record who now have a difficult time being accepted back into society. Such individuals require housing, practical vocational education, assistance with job placement, help to overcome addictions, and most important, those who will love and point them to Christ.

Do we realize how many in the world today are in need of some simple skills that we may take for granted? They include how to manage finances, computer/Internet literacy, workplace etiquette, how to prepare a résumé, how to dress for an interview, and how to do a sales call—and the list goes on and on. Some cities could use ESL (English as a second language) classes. One approach would be to have such a home located outside of the city and train people how to farm and grow their own food as a basis for getting back on their feet. After researching the varied corporate, professional, and labor skills among local Seventh-day Adventists, your church could begin planning a full-time "workingmen's home." Many of our own church members actually need simple job skills themselves, so they too could stand to benefit. Start with your own congregation and neighborhood and see what happens. As we provide a place that men and women could look to for help, our local community would see something that Christ longs to do through us.

A Bath Establishment

In the original Beehive vision in San Francisco the St. Helena Sanitarium operated a branch near City Hall in downtown San Francisco. The reason they did so was quite simple. Few would ever hear about or look for a place to restore and rejuvenate their health located 90 minutes outside of the city. Yet many working in the midst of the city, recognizing their need for relief from stress or a boost to their health, will seek a local health spa. St. Helena Sanitarium established its branch as a place where people could receive hydrotherapy, massage therapy, and more, yet was only blocks away from their place of business or residence in downtown San Francisco.

"I have been given light that in many cities it is advisable for a restaurant to be connected with treatment rooms. The two can cooperate in upholding right principles. In connection with these it is sometimes advisable to have rooms that will serve as lodgings for the sick. These establishments will serve as feeders to the sanitariums located in the country and would better be conducted in rented buildings. We are not to erect in the cities large buildings in which to care for the sick, because God has plainly indicated that the sick can be better cared for outside of the cities. In many places it will be necessary to begin sanitarium work in the cities; but, as much as possible, this work should be transferred to the country as soon as suitable locations can be secured" (*Testimonies for the Church,* vol. 7, p. 60).

A small health spa would most closely resemble the bath establishment of yesteryear. Offering massage, saunas, hydrotherapy, and other natural health-rejuvenating services, it would be a great way to encourage people on their way to better health. The city spa could serve as a "feeder" to the health resort (outpost) outside of the city for those in need of greater health rejuvenation.

Doctors and Dentists and Medical Practitioners

Physicians were intimately involved with the program in San Francisco. Ellen G. White wrote that "Dr. and Mrs. Dr. Lamb are doing much medical work for the poor in connection with their regular practice; and Dr. Buchannan is doing much free work at the Workingmen's Home" (in Australasian *Union Conference Record,* Mar. 1, 1901).

Today many Seventh-day Adventist physicians have talents and expertise the people of our cities are in desperate need of. Such professionals should consider doing the kinds of things that earlier Adventists did for the poor of San Francisco. Today it could involve more than offering free medical services—it could also include free classes offered by respected professionals.

Imagine a local doctor's office sending out postcards to the community and offering them a class on how to prevent diabetes or reduce blood sugar or find better ways to sleep. As the health-care crisis gets worse and worse, it will lead to still greater need for practical health education in the great cities of the world. It is not because of lack of access to health care or lack of money, but because people simply don't know that lifestyle and dietary choices directly contribute to the majority of the diseases that plague the world today.

Any physician or dentist can open their office or give of their time to educate the community, and it will produce a twofold blessing. The first is that it will educate people in regard to lifestyle and its relation to their physical, mental, and spiritual health. The second is that they will perceive doctors as a blessing to the needy and as people who desire the good health of the community. It was what Christ was known for, and we can share the same reputation today.

DISCUSSION BREAKOUT SESSION WORKSHEET

Assignment 1

As a group, list five observations about the three concepts we have been discussing.

_____

_____

Assignment 2

As a group, list the harsh realities or characteristics that can cause such programs to falter. Which ones are common among all three concepts?

_____

_____

Assignment 3

Discuss and list what steps must be taken to correct such problems.

_____

_____

Assignment 4

What steps would your group take to make recommendations to those seeking to implement each concept to help the group avoid total failure?

_____

_____

CHAPTER 5

THE RESURRECTION IN ATLANTA

During late 2008, with the approaching "year of evangelism" being planned by the General Conference in preparation for its session scheduled for the summer of 2010, a few key figures of the Beehive were just looking for ways to jump-start evangelism in Atlanta, where they sought to hold a series of traditional evangelism meetings in 2009. And thus the journey commenced.

As the time to begin the meetings approached, their intense study began to uncover the secrets to successful evangelism. They used the book *Evangelism,* by Ellen G. White, and it made deep impressions on their minds regarding the kinds of meeting places they should employ, correct methods of follow-up, and the value of ongoing Bible studies with people contacted directly. It was clear that true success would come by following God's blueprint for evangelism.

At an early-morning Bible study at an Adventist man's business in Atlanta, several men began brainstorming about a location to hold meetings. After walking back from breakfast, the group noticed a particular vacant store. Approximately 14,000 square feet in size, it was quite a bit more than what the brainstorming session had envisioned, but they decided to investigate whether God was leading them to this location.

They offered prayer right there in front of the retail space. What followed was a ridiculous proposal to the owner to rent the 14,000-square-foot space for $1,000 per month. It is important to note that the space typically went for $14,000-$20,000 per month.

Of course everyone agreed that it was a crazy offer, but they also felt that God was leading. Each had a strong impression that God was about to do something special.

The Lord did not disappoint. Without blinking or haggling, the owner accepted the offer. God had given evidence that it was time to go out on a limb for Him—to take risks and leave the details up to Him. After giving prayers of thanksgiving, the leaders decided that the first meeting would begin in 30 days.

Some, who were on the outside looking in, observed that it was indeed presumption. It would take nothing short of a miracle to get the place ready in 30 days. The store had a bare floor that had missing tiles where store shelves had once been. Electrical wiring hung everywhere, and the walls were damaged. It was 14,000 square feet of complete mess.

But then the miracles started happening. First, donors who were willing to contribute time and/or money stepped up. The place badly needed carpet, yet to cover 14,000 square feet of floor space was going to be cost-prohibitive. But God is always faithful. The group found a closeout sale on carpets and, by God's providence, it was just enough. It was so close that they had only enough left over for a doormat.

BP-2

The walls needed repair and paint, so God sent volunteers. They came from several different congregations, and it was busy—much like the early Beehive churches in San Francisco and Oakland during Ellen White's day. But with all of this work being done, they had no way to financially take care of all of the needed electrical work. But on the first official workday, God sent a skilled and faithful local church member who was a wonderful help as he provided countless hours of electrical service work.

About nine days before the big opening night, while doing touch-up painting, the sense of accomplishment was thick in the air. The finish line was in sight. As the group made final touches it appeared that the tremendous amount of work was winding up. They had built a new stage, the carpet had been ordered for it, and that would be it. Then it happened. The fire marshal came in and stated that they needed some fire caulking as well as a full inspection of the space. It was as if God Himself had announced, "I've changed My mind. Thanks for the hard work, but you can go home now." It felt as though the world had ended. But, remembering how far the Lord had brought things and had blessed at every single step, they decided that it was a test and that the work must go forward.

So the group had to jump through more and more hoops to meet current building codes. According to recent building code changes, the space was out-of-date, and many items had to be upgraded. A surprise blessing came when the owner agreed to assist financially.

The fire marshal was doing his best to be helpful, but he could hardly contain himself when he found out that the opening night was less than a week away. While he admired the effort, courage, and optimism, he still said that there was "no way" the group could meet all the code requirements in such a short time. He felt that it would take a miracle. Little did he know that those were all the words God needed him to speak.

After calling for a final inspection, the fire marshal informed them that in order to be able to seat 800 people, they would need an additional exit door. Later they learned that in discussions with the other marshals he had said, "Well, they gave it a try, but they won't make it." Another city fire chief had replied, "Don't plan on that—those men have God on their side."

The days and nights were long all the way up to opening night. A number of people even worked through the night to get everything done. After 19 straight days everyone was exhausted. But God is faithful and promises to be always with His people, to give them help and strength.

On that final day the fire marshal, who didn't believe in miracles, had his belief system challenged. Absolutely astonished when he came for the final inspection and saw everything completed, he gave the approval. God had blessed, and the meetings would begin right there in that large, well-known retail plaza next to a popular Atlanta restaurant. What had happened wasn't about the fire marshal or those who were doing the work, but what God will do with a committed few and how He was preparing to give the last message of warning in the cities through a little-known concept called the Beehive. We had witnessed the resurrection of integrated personal evangelism.

From February of 2009 through October of 2009 some activity was going on nearly every weekend. Revival meetings, Bible studies, health seminars, cooking classes, and prophecy meetings, as well as many other events, were conducted. A number of people requested home visits, and studies with those who had no church affiliation began.

Even a Muslim family came to the health seminars and immediately wanted to start doing Bible studies. It was amazing to watch God work.

As a result of the meetings a number of church members expressed a desire to learn how health can be an opening door to meet people and lead them to Christ. So a three-month program was set up on the premises to train individuals in what is typically known as "medical missionary" programs. A number of those who participated in the classes have gone on to minister in local churches and to the community at large. It will become abundantly clearer that medical missionary training and activities are critical to the Beehive process of reaching the cities.

After the team had witnessed all of God's blessings and assurances that it was His ministry, they wondered if they could replicate it elsewhere. After prayerful consideration the team began plans to launch the next phase in Arizona, under the name The Beehive. It did not take long before it became abundantly clear that the Lord was leading and that the Beehive concept was much more than they had initially comprehended. While God had revealed much, He was also showing us that we had still more to learn. But it was obvious that the Bcchive could be duplicated anywhere God's people are willing to follow His instructions implicitly and to go wherever people are who need to know Jesus.

"As I see what the Lord has wrought, I am filled with astonishment, and with confidence in Christ as leader. We have nothing to fear for the future, except as we shall forget the way the Lord has led us, and His teaching in our past history" (*Counsels for the Church*, p. 359).

DISCUSSION BREAKOUT SESSION WORKSHEET

Assignment 1

As a group, discuss each of the nine Beehive components in detail.

_____

_____

Assignment 2

Keeping in mind the ministries in your local church as well as local ministries and businesses in your area, discuss how easy or difficult implementing any of the various facets of the Beehive would be. How will they work together? Be exhaustive and detailed.

_____

_____

Assignment 3

Using a dry-erase board or flipcharts, discuss a strategic plan for implementing one, some, or all of the Beehive ministries.

_____

_____

Assignment 4

Again, using the dry-erase board, draw a time line and establish a time frame for implementing your town's or city's Beehive.

_____

_____

Assignment 5

As a group, set real goals for your Beehive. Make revival and reformation, training, and evangelism a part of your goals.

_____

_____

CHAPTER 6

THE MIRROR: "CASE STUDIES"

I n this chapter we will examine a few case studies to illustrate the various factors and principles involved in setting up a Beehive structure. Rather than use churches as examples (which may strike too close to home), we will instead employ other types of organizations, such as business companies, etc. They should make for interesting group discussion. Carefully make a full analysis of each case, being sure to pay attention to the principles that affect the organization either negatively or positively.

Fortune 500 Company

Let's imagine a Fortune 500 company that we'll call "We Makc Money." Having more than 10,000 employees occupying 10 floors in a downtown skyscraper, it is located in a large city. The organization is quite proud of its charter: "We exist for no other purpose than to make lots of money for our stockholders." A few years prior they had issued a most impressive annual report, which detailed shrewd and gutsy acquisitions, global sales that were through the roof, and new products that were second to none. However, We Make Money held a lot of big, expensive parties, continually patted itself on the back, and dove deep into a sea of complacency. It no longer introduced any new products, because it had cut back on recruiting new talent, preferring to look in-house for new ideas, and it had cut the research and development budget 80 percent. Now the company was operating in the red and losing market share. The stockholders were getting anxious. What should We Make Money do?

Athletic Team

A basketball franchise has the most dynamic and expensive sports arena of its kind. It is elaborate, replete with luxury boxes to boot. The team's uniforms are top-notch. They have the most loyal fans imaginable. Everyone feels that they are a part of the club. The team (we'll call them "We Win Games") has a strong and deep legacy of being the franchise you can always count on. After winning two championships back to back, they slashed the recruitment budget. After all, they had honestly earned their nickname, "The Invincibles." Furthermore, they now had to help pay for the new arena. But the club had quite a mascot. Fans went crazy over the high-flying, dunking personification of "The Invincibles."

Meanwhile, the league's trend of literally searching the world over for the tallest and most skilled players became the norm. But not so with We Win Games. They instead depended on their old players, opting to save time and money since this team had proved itself twice. Unfortunately it now has not won any games during the past two seasons, and their loyal fans have become a little sick of buying season tickets for a losing team. What should We Win Games do?

National Restaurant Chain

The "Best Veggie Burgers Ever" has 1,200 franchised stores throughout the world. The interior design of the store is amazing and immaculate. When you walk into the restaurant, the decor and use of vibrant colors immediately stimulate the salivary glands to the extent that you're twice as hungry as you were before you entered. It was common knowledge that they had the best veggie burger in town. Yes, the best veggie burger. They sold only one type. But then a competitor opened up and went directly after them, strategically placing a burger joint down the street from each of their locations. What's more, they copied their recipe, offered five new veggie burgers, and added cheese and pickles. It cut Best Veggie Burgers' business in half. In a panic, they attempted to slow the hemorrhaging and regain market share by offering 17 different types of veggie burgers. Their motto became "A Veggie Burger for Your Every Whim—or Else." Unfortunately, the move divided the management into different factions, since no one could agree on which items were good and which ones were bad. Well, if someone didn't like the taste of the new veggie burger, the "or else" became "receive a full refund," "stay at home," "go to the competition," or "throw them at the cashier." Best Veggie Burgers Ever was causing sleepless nights for the owners/franchisees as their sales plummeted precipitously. What should Best Veggie Burgers Ever do?

Here we have three examples of organizations that are not living up to the mission set forth in their incorporation documents. Sure, the examples are silly, but in some instances not too far from the truth. A few sports teams have even ended up with winless seasons. However, when such things happen, out of responsibility to its stockholders, fans, or customers, the organization will take immediate steps to correct the problem. Let's pause here and allow the case studies to invoke some discussion to determine what should be done to get such organizations back on track.

(In every other instance we have held any discussions at the end of the chapter. It is important here, however, to have a discussion interlude. You may be tempted to skip ahead for answers and the observations about the Beehive concept, but resist it. God wants you to arrive at your own conclusions through prayer and discussion. You can learn much from considering such examples, even if they are secular ones. As Jesus observed: "The children of this world are in their generation wiser than the children of light" [Luke 16:8].)

You have prayerfully considered in detail the three organizations—the good, the bad, and everything in between. We are now ready to press forward, now equipped with your thoughts and lists of observations, along with these below.

Characteristics of the three organizations:
1. They became complacent.
2. They rested on yesterday's success.
3. They drifted away from what made them successful in the beginning.

4. They invested in things rather than people.
5. They conformed to the competition instead of holding to core values.
6. They allowed a problem to go on for too long.
7. They more than likely ignored input from managers, employees, and customers.
8. They got so comfortable that they became clubs unto themselves.
9. They did not anticipate change and the need for innovation.
10. They lost their unity.
11. As a result, all three were obviously failing.

Perhaps in your group discussion you arrived at more conclusions. That is entirely possible. But the above are the main issues that have created problems for these three organizations. Now let's look at how to tackle the problem.

Clearly, if such organizations are to continue to exist, they will have to deal head-on with such problems. What is the first order of business? Here's our list:

1. Take an honest look at where the organization is and admit failure.
2. Devise a plan to identify clearly what problems are the root causes. Is it a personnel problem, a lost sight of mission, a lack of business strategy, a misappropriation of funds/finances, external forces (i.e., competition), etc.?
3. Carefully revisit the mission, charter, or bylaws of the organization.
4. Strategize to reinstate the core values and mission of the organization.
5. Allocate funds to implement the strategy.
6. Execute the strategy.

Were your observations and conclusions similar to the ones above? Based on your group's observations and the answers provided here, how quickly should the organization adopt the conclusions reached to avoid going out of business? Can you imagine operating in the red (not making a profit but continuing business as usual), especially when the name of your organization is We Make Money? How about your basketball team proudly saying to the world, "We win games," when it has not won any for two years? Should it continue the celebrations from two years ago? Finally, what if you sell veggie burgers and no one likes them and therefore avoids your restaurant like the plague, but your name proclaims that you have the "best veggie burgers ever"? How long should the organization continue to add new gimmicks to attract its customers back before they just return to what worked in the past?

No organization of the world worth its salt would ever, upon arriving at the conclusion that it is no longer accomplishing the task for which it was started, then continue business as usual. According to Einstein, doing the same thing but expecting different results is insanity. Most corporations have consulting firms on retainer who conduct research monthly, quarterly, or annually to show the organization where they are at all times. It is a health check, so to speak. The moment that sales dip, businesses conduct analyses to determine where the problem lies. In fact, most successful organizations won't even wait until then. They are constantly studying trends, carefully forecasting, and planning and developing new strategies and products to remain relevant in the marketplace. They measure everything against their best practices and core competencies and practices (that which they do well). Never deviating from the organization's mission, lest the stockholders or fans revolt, successful businesses have always taken an honest look at themselves and how they are performing against their stated goals. They have an obligation not only to the owner or owners but also to those who are looking to them for the services they provide.

Now, let's look at your church. Perhaps it is filled to capacity. Praise the Lord! But that would put your church in the minority category. Most churches (at least in North America and parts of Europe) have memberships that are dwindling at an alarming pace. We are not retaining those who are baptized. It is no secret that they come in and then go back out. If we did a case study on the Adventist Church, we would also refer to it as an organization. By the way, the church is the greatest organization on earth, as God ordained and organized it Himself. We should give our organization a name also, following the same pattern of the previous case studies. All you need to do is add SDA after it. Here are some names to choose from (or you can make up your own):

1. "We Go Where People Are"
2. "We Live the Truth"
3. "Souls Saved Here"
4. "New Lives Born Daily"
5. "Love and Warmth Live Here"
6. "The All-Are-Welcome House"
7. "The Lost Are Found Here"
8. "We Are Sinners; We Welcome Others"

This case study will be brief, as we can appropriately apply the previous principles of failure. Let's use "We Go Where People Are," a title based on the very words of Christ when He said, "Go ye therefore." This church used to be full to capacity. You even had to come to Sabbath school early or you wouldn't get a seat at the 11:00 service. Evangelism was the heartbeat of the church and its membership. But something happened. The congregation has not had a baptism in five years. No new members have even transferred. Some members listed on the membership rolls have not been to church in 20 years. A few names on the membership records are even now resting in their graves. The young adults have all left, so there are now no new families (no need for cradle roll). The church is half full, however, and the potlucks are always exquisite. So despite the lack of growth, everyone seems happy with the status of the church, and things go on as "normal."

Here's the question: Are the children of the world wiser than the children of light? Sure, Jesus asked the question. But He raised it because through a parable He was teaching a principle that His church must always be mindful of. Jesus was always looking down through the ages with a prophetic eye on His church. He also said that the harvest would be ripe, but the laborers would be few. It was not a statement of acceptance any more than the one that the world would do things wiser than His people. God wants His church to avoid this trap. In other words, it was a warning of what could eventually happen. So He gave instruction as to what to do should it happen: let us pray to the Lord of harvest and make friends.

How is it that the organizations of the world will do health checks, conduct surveys and market research, and make adjustments when they are no longer living up to their mission and objectives, but the church of the living God, the organization that He has placed in human hands and given the Holy Spirit to be its guide, will do less than that of secular entities?

Friends, we must take an honest look at ourselves and pray to God for the help that He longs to bestow upon His remnant church. If we are not accomplishing the goals and living up to the standard that He set for His church, then we are failing. In the business world identifying failure is not a source of shame and condemnation. Better to know where things are than not. If we say that our goal is to win people to Christ and we're not doing it, we're failing. No need to hang our heads. Instead, we need to discuss how to get back to the blueprint. If we say that we are a loving church, but people join and then don't stay, we have come short of what we have advertised. Again, there is no need to feel condemned. Count it all joy when the Lord holds up the mirror to show us where we are erring. It is an act of His mercy. We cannot be so right that we cannot accept our wrongs.

In this chapter we have presented a lighthearted approach to seeing ourselves as we really are, one utilizing case studies, a practice often employed as a learning exercise during seminars and within business schools. We have analyzed what things make a worldly organization fail, and built upon the argument that they will not continue the same course when obvious failure is apparent. Hopefully you discussed as a group your collective insights as how to turn that organization around. Our prayer is that it was a lively discussion and that you have learned much about how to correct our course when things are going badly. In the process we moved from the levity of discussing the worldly organizations to looking rather seriously at our church (not anyone else's, but ours) and concluded that we, like those hypothetical organizations, need to apply principles that will change our course. The case studies should help you to continue the discussion as you consider how critical it was to transform the secular businesses, and then use that same fervor and determination to change the course of our own local congregation. Continue to pray as you discuss.

DISCUSSION BREAKOUT SESSION WORKSHEET

Please begin with a word of prayer, inviting the Holy Spirit into your discussion. Then have each member answer the following questions: What is the greatest partnership the universe has ever known? Why does it work?

Assignment 1

Have each individual in your group select from the Bible examples of partnerships formed to further God's purposes. Share the examples with the rest of the group and discuss the principles you find in them.

_____

_____

Assignment 2

List a few secular partnerships or mergers reported in the media or that you've noticed. What reasons do you think such partnerships formed in the first place? Based on what you know, are the partnerships working? Why or why not?

_____

_____

Assignment 3

Split your group in half. Have one group list some of the pitfalls or challenges of partnerships. Have the other half of the group itemize the benefits. Come up with as many examples as you can. Then discuss as a group how to use biblical principles to overcome obstacles that they might face. Likewise, discuss how to accentuate and grow the benefits.

_____

_____

Assignment 4

List the current ways that your church has formed partnerships. For example, first list how the ministries within your church have found ways to get more done by uniting forces. In other words, do the Sabbath schools work with the personal ministries department to do outreach? Is the young adults ministry partnering with the health ministries to do community health surveys? Then list how your church may have currently found partnerships outside of your congregation.

_____

_____

CHAPTER 7

CENTERS OF INFLUENCE

t is always best to endeavor to carry out the whole will of God as He has specified. He will take care of the results" (*Medical Ministry,* p. 256).

What Ellen White called "centers of influence" in the Bay Area during her time comprised 14 different programs that Adventists used to reach those two cities. For the purposes of the Beehive setup of our current day we have culled them down basically to nine areas, with others being subsets of the nine. All nine should work synergistically with each other and make up one Beehive organization, whether they all start at once or gradually through time.

In this section we will show the core essentials in each facet of the nine as well as their relationships. While it is best to have all nine facets functioning at the same time, every planned Beehive must commence somewhere, and not everyone can start with the nine operating from the outset. However, everyone should understand that a Beehive ministry is uniquely multifaceted, requiring collective lines of missionary activity. Thus, when starting a Beehive, you should enter into it prayerfully with the intent to develop all parts of it and have all of them functioning in your city or town. Below is the suggested outline or order of the various ministry components to a Beehive setup, based on practical considerations, research, and experience:

1. **Ministry of the churches: the launching pad/training center**
   a. Revival and reformation meetings
   b. The hub of all activity

2. **Ministry of health and reform: retraining members and hearts**
   a. Physical and spiritual revival through health improvement
   b. Character development
   c. Missionary training with emphasis on the development of a servant's heart

3. **Ministry of house-to-house labor/gospel workers**
   a. Medical missionary/health evangelist
      1. Conduct health surveys
      2. Form groups to work the city
      3. Conduct health seminars
      4. Visit the sick

     5. Teach health principles

     6. Conduct cooking classes

  b. Literature evangelist

     1. Conduct health surveys

     2. Distribute/sell literature

  c. Bible instructor

     1. Conduct health surveys

     2. Obtain interest for Bible studies

4. **Ministry to the rich: integrated evangelism**
   a. Conduct health surveys
   b. Conduct health seminars
   c. Conduct cooking classes

5. **Ministry to the poor: integrated evangelism**
   a. Community centers
   b. Food banks
   c. "Workmen's home" = train/assist the unemployed

6. **Ministry of food science: integrated evangelism**
   a. Restaurant
   b. Health food stores
   c. Health spas
   d. Cooking classes and demonstrations

7. **Ministry of lifestyle reform/outpost health resorts: integrated evangelism**
   a. Set up country outposts
   b. Conduct 21-day lifestyle programs
      1. Stop Smoking program
      2. Reverse Diabetes program
      3. Depression Recovery program
      4. Total body cleanses
   c. Staff training for city missions
   d. Set up agricultural training

8. **Ministry of integrated personal evangelism**
   Conduct evangelistic programs

9. **Ministry to the prisons**
   Set up prison ministry

SECTION 1:
Ministry of the Churches: the Launching Pad/Training Center

We will first look at the ministry that the churches are responsible for. According to *A Call to Medical Evangelism and Health Education,* "every church should be a training school for Christian workers" (p. 18). It is at this critical and foundational stage that the Beehive concept must be initiated as a partnership with the local congregation. Many congregations have lost the evangelistic zeal necessary for the growth and health of the body of Christ. Some do an amazing job of caring for the flock already in the fold, but no longer have a passion for those outside it. Here is where the Beehive concept comes in. Without disrupting the pastoral care of the flock, it becomes the training, revival, reformation, and evangelistic arm of the local congregation. It doesn't become a new church but gives the congregation a "dual" engine, bringing the balance missing from so many churches. The key is to establish a Beehive partnership with the local congregation. But first, let's examine the Ministry of the Churches section, as we build on the Beehive concept to reach the cities.

Inspiration reminds us that "enfeebled and defective as it may appear, the church is the one object upon which God bestows in a special sense His supreme regard. It is the theater of His grace, in which He delights to reveal His power to transform hearts" (*The Acts of the Apostles,* p. 12).

Proverbs 6:6 invites us to study the ant: "Go to the ant, thou sluggard, consider her ways, and be wise." If an object lesson exists in an ant, can we say the same thing of the bee and its hive?

The Beehive

The characteristics of a beehive are truly fascinating. Here are just a few facts:
1. Bees fill the hive at all times.
2. A beehive is a busy center of productive activity.
3. A beehive is strong and formidable.
4. A beehive has many members with different roles working in unison.
5. A beehive is highly organized, nurturing, and protective.
6. A beehive provides and even sacrifices for its leader (the queen of the colony).
7. A beehive's success and viability depend upon the worker bees' usefulness beyond the confines of the hive. The bees don't stay within the hive but actively range beyond it.

Could God's church embrace and replicate the characteristics of a beehive? It did in the early 1900s, and it must do so today in order to reach the cities with the three angels' messages. What we present here is not an untested method, but rather one with strong effectiveness.

The Messenger's Vision

"During the past few years the 'beehive' in San Francisco has been indeed a busy one. Many lines of Christian effort have been carried forward by our brethren and sisters there" (*Welfare Ministry,* p. 112).

Characteristics of the Apostolic Church

- *Depended* on God as it organized—"And they prayed, and said, Thou, Lord, which knowest the hearts of all men, show whether of these two thou hast chosen, that he may take part of this ministry and apostleship" (Acts 1:24, 25).
- *Prayed* in unity—"These all continued with one accord in prayer and supplication" (verse 14). "They were all with one accord in one place" (Acts 2:1). "And they, continuing daily with one accord in the temple . . ." (verse 46).
- *Experienced* constant growth—"And the same day there were added unto them about three thousand souls" (verse 41). "And the Lord added to the church daily such as should be saved" (verse 47). "Many of them which heard the word believed; and the number of the men was about five thousand" (Acts 4:4).
- *Continued* a medical missionary spirit—Peter commands a lame man to walk (Acts 3:6). "And many taken with palsies, and that were lame, were healed" (Act 8:7). "And Peter said . . . , Aeneas, Jesus Christ maketh thee whole: arise, and make thy bed. And he rose immediately" (Acts 9:34). We can also look back to the time when they were all with Christ and He gave them directions for their success. We see in Luke 9 and 10 that He commanded the Twelve and then the 70 both to preach and to heal the sick.
- *Practiced* visitation — "And breaking bread from house to house . . ." (Acts 2:46).
- *Evangelized house to house*—"But have shewed you, and taught you . . . house to house" (Acts 20:20). "And in every house, they ceased not to teach and preach Jesus Christ" (Acts 5:42).
- *Evangelized publicly*—"But have shewed you, and have taught you publicly" (Acts 20:20).
- *Gave* sacrificially—"And sold their possessions and goods, and parted them to all men" (Acts 2:45).
- *Ministered* to the needy—"And parted [their goods and possessions] to all men, as every man had need" (verse 45). "Then the disciples, every man according to his ability, determined to send relief unto the brethren which dwelt in Judaea" (Acts 11:29).
- *Fearlessly* faced opposition—"Certain Jews from Antioch and Iconium . . . stoned Paul, drew him out of the city, supposing he had been dead" (Acts 14:19). But they did so without fear—"And when they had preached the gospel to that city [Derbe)] and had taught many, they returned again to Lystra, and to Iconium, and Antioch" (verse 21). Regarding the experiences in Antioch and Iconium, the prophet of the Lord writes: "But they by no means took final leave; they purposed to return after the excitement had abated, and complete the work begun" (*The Acts of the Apostles,* p. 179). "And so, undaunted by danger, 'they returned again to Lystra, and to Iconium, and Antioch, confirming the souls of the disciples, and exhorting them to continue in the faith'" (*ibid.,* p. 185).

Apostolic Succession

"So the apostolic succession rests not upon the transmission of ecclesiastical authority, but upon spiritual relationship. A life actuated by the apostles' spirit, the belief and teaching of the truth they taught, this is the true evidence of apostolic succession. This is what constitutes men the successors of the first teachers of the gospel" (*The Desire of Ages,* p. 467).

And Today . . .

"The cause of God in the earth today is in need of living representatives of Bible truth. The ordained ministers alone are not equal to the task of warning the great cities. God is calling not only upon ministers, but also upon physicians, nurses, colporteurs, Bible workers, and other consecrated laymen of varied talent who have a knowledge of the word of God and who know the power of His grace, to consider the needs of the unwarned cities" (*The Acts of the Apostles,* pp. 158, 159).

Truly the idea of the Beehive did not begin with a dream in the nineteenth century. From the Bible we see the very DNA of the Beehive existing in apostolic times. The Beehive idea—integrated personal evangelism—demonstrated itself in the lives of the apostles. As did Jesus, they ministered to the needs of the poor and exhibited the gift of healing, using health as an entering wedge. They spent time in people's homes, sharing the love of Jesus. Always, they went to where the people were.

The Church-Beehive Partnership

The Beehive concept is not a new church but engages, equips, and empowers local church members to embrace revival and reformation in preparation for reaching the cities through the other eight aspects of the Beehive city mission.

The ministry of churches aspect lies at the center of the Beehive. It is where everything begins, the launching pad for revival and reformation. Those who are deepening their relational walk with Christ and desire to be colaborers with Him will ultimately take a decided interest and be trained effectively in the Beehive system. The people of God must experience a longing to reach cities. This is where the heart change must take place. Then and only then will the members be able to share the gospel in the wicked cities of the world.

"Shall we not do all in our power to advance the work in all of our large cities? Thousands upon thousands who live near us need help in various ways. Let the ministers of the gospel remember that the Lord Jesus Christ said to His disciples: 'Ye are the light of the world. A city that is set on a hill cannot be hid.' . . . Matthew 5:14" (*Testimonies for the Church,* vol. 7, p. 114).

Every large city in the world should have a Beehive operating in partnership with the local congregations and existing ministries.

"And that, knowing the time, that *now* it is high time to awake out of sleep: for now is our salvation nearer than when we believed" (Rom. 13:11).

"Thou therefore, my son, be strong in the grace that is in Christ Jesus. And the things that thou hast heard of me among many witnesses, the same commit thou to faithful men, who shall be able to teach others also. Thou therefore endure hardness, as a good soldier of Jesus Christ" (2 Tim. 2:1-3).

So a Beehive center in every city is the first step to begin the work of training churches.

"The church of Christ is organized for service. Its watchword is ministry. Its members are soldiers, to be trained for conflict under the Captain of their salvation" (*A Call to Medical Evangelism and Health Education,* p. 17).

"The monotony of our service for God needs to be broken up. Every church member should be engaged in some line of service for the Master. Some cannot do so much as others, but everyone should do his utmost to roll back the tide of disease and distress that is sweeping over our world. Many would be willing to work if they were taught how to begin. They need to be instructed and encouraged" (*ibid.*).

"Every church should be a training school for Christian workers. Its members should be taught how to give Bible readings, how to conduct and teach Sabbath school classes, how best to help the poor and to care for the sick, how to work for the unconverted. There should be schools of health, cooking schools, and classes in various lines of Christian help work. There should not only be teaching, but actual work under experienced instructors. Let the teachers lead the way in working among the people, and others, uniting with them, will learn from their example. One example is worth more than many precepts" (*The Ministry of Healing*, p. 149).

The Beehive concept will work with local congregations and ministries, uniting their various activities and training their members how to teach, lead, and serve by example, all within the multifaceted Beehive framework. Truly, the Lord has given a beautiful structure to this concept. If followed, we believe it will accomplish the intended goal of preparing the cities for the coming of the Lord. We will outline in practical details the simple steps in the following sections.

This Beehive blueprint manual serves as a guide to getting started and beginning the process of involving members in reaching the cities. It seeks to offer practical training and informational resources, serving as a connector and networker for other Beehive partnerships throughout the world.

"There is need of coming close to the people by personal effort. If less time were given to sermonizing, and more time were spent in personal ministry, greater results would be seen" (*ibid.,* p. 143).

Christ approached the people so that He might heal and comfort them and speak to them of the higher spiritual life. How can we do that in our religiously intolerant world? This is the very heart and essence of the Beehive—integrated personal evangelism.

SECTION 2:
Ministry of Health and Reform:
Retraining Members and Hearts

It may seem a bit premature to deal with health. After all, the previous section focused primarily with the local congregation and its need for trained members. Shouldn't the first training be how to give Bible studies? Perhaps the distribution of literature will bring us into close contact with the people. But Christ had a method. It alone will successfully reach the people of the cities. Taking a personal approach, getting close to the people, He won their confidence. We can think of no greater ways to win the confidence of an individual than to care for someone who is sick, provide food for someone who is hungry, or offer shelter to someone who is homeless. As we continue to build on the Beehive concept, we will illustrate how the Lord has shown that the health and healing approach is critical for our churches to reach the cities. But probably not for the reasons you would think—at least not initially.

Reading the writings of Ellen G. White you will often see the term *medical missionary* or *medical missionary work*. In fact, she repeatedly refers to Christ as the great medical missionary. It is an old and probably even archaic term often employed during the 1800s. A brief look into denominational history will show that *medical missionary* was not the term first used. Rather, Adventists spoke of "benevolent work" as well as "Christian help work." As a result one can begin to see something more than medical in the expression. In other words, it was a work of benevolence or "well-doing," of Christians helping those less fortunate and in need. It does not exclude those who may have been sick or suffering from some disease, of course, but it involved more than just the medical side of things.

The term really found its place in the Seventh-day Adventist Church in large part because of the case of Hannah More, whom Ellen White wrote about in *Testimonies for the Church* (vol. 1, pp. 666-680; vol. 2, pp. 140-145, 332; vol. 3, pp. 407, 408). In short, the early church in Battle Creek, Michigan, did not take in this aging Christian missionary, and Ellen White sternly reproved the congregation for the neglect. She states plainly:

"In the case of Sister Hannah More, I was shown that the neglect of her was the neglect of Jesus in her person. Had the Son of God come in the humble, unpretending manner in which He journeyed from place to place when He was upon earth, He would have met with no better reception" (*ibid.*, vol. 2, p. 140).

Notice that what she does is really a shining of the lesser light on the greater, illumined principle outlined in Matthew 25:40, in which Christ points out what separates the sheep from the goats: "Inasmuch as ye have done it unto one of the least of these . . ." When Hannah More (one of the least) could find no Adventist home to take her in, it exposed the heart of the Adventist congregation in Battle Creek. Notice especially what Ellen White says next: "It is the deep principle of love that dwelt in the bosom of the humble Man of Calvary that is needed" (*ibid.*, vol. 2, p. 140).

She hones in on the very core issue—the heart. It was "the deep principle of love," Christ's love, that the people of Battle Creek lacked. It led to Hannah More leaving the fellowship of Adventists in Battle Creek to stay with non-Sabbathkeepers in another part of Michigan, where she found only a place in a chimney-exhaust-filled attic and quickly contracted tuberculosis and died. (You can and should read the entire account in the first three volumes of the *Testimonies*.)

The case of Hannah More led the Seventh-day Adventist Church to embrace the "Benevolent Work," which laid the foundation for what later became the medical missionary program. This manual will refer to it as gospel medical missionary work, sometimes interchangeably with lifestyle education and health evangelism. There are two reasons that we are comfortable using the term *medical missionary*. First, Ellen White spoke of Christ as "the great medical missionary . . . our example" (*Christian Service,* p. 133), and second, she states that Satan will at the very end come "pretending to be the great medical missionary"

(*Medical Ministry,* p. 87). Therefore the term *medical missionary* has end-time significance, which is why we will continue to use it as it relates to the health and healing program for reaching the cities.

Since Ellen White refers to Christ as the great medical missionary who is our example, it clearly shows that the idea did not just begin with the case of Hannah More. Her experience merely revived it. This is important to understand in an end-time context. But first, let's look at some examples, as seen in Scripture and the writings of Ellen G. White.

Christ

"And Jesus went about all the cities and villages, teaching in their synagogues, and preaching the gospel of the kingdom, and healing every sickness and every disease among the people" (Matt. 9:35).

"Christ has given us an example. He taught from the Scriptures the gospel truths, and He also healed the afflicted ones who came to Him for relief. He was the greatest physician the world ever knew, and yet He combined with His healing work the imparting of soul-saving truth" (*A Call to Medical Evangelism and Health Education,* p. 27).

"Christ sought the people where they were, and placed before them the great truths in regard to His kingdom. As He went from place to place, He blessed and comforted the suffering and healed the sick. This is our work. God would have us relieve the necessities of the destitute. The reason that the Lord does not manifest His power more decidedly is because there is so little spirituality among those who claim to believe the truth" (*Medical Ministry,* p. 319).

"How slow men are to understand God's preparation for the day of His power. He works today to reach hearts in the same way that He worked when Christ was upon this earth. In reading the Word of God, we see that Christ brought medical missionary work into His ministry. Cannot our eyes be opened to discern Christ's methods? Cannot we understand the commission He gave to His disciples and to us?" (*A Call to Medical Evangelism and Health Education,* p. 12).

The Apostles

Peter—"Then Peter said, Silver and gold have I none; but such as I have give I thee: In the name of Jesus Christ of Nazareth rise up and walk" (Acts 3:6).

Philip—"Then Philip went down to the city of Samaria, and preached Christ unto them. And the people with one accord gave heed unto those things which Philip spake, hearing and seeing the miracles which he did. For unclean spirits, crying with loud voice, came out of many that were possessed with them: and many taken with palsies, and that were lame, were healed" (Acts 8:5-7).

Paul—"The same heard Paul speak: who stedfastly beholding him, and perceiving that he had faith to be healed, said with a loud voice, Stand upright on thy feet. And he leaped and walked" (Acts 14:9, 10).

We find a powerful lesson on medical missionary activity recorded in the story of Publius. It shows that first-century Christians used it wherever they were, even when shipwrecked.

"And it came to pass, that the father of Publius lay sick of a fever and of a bloody flux: to whom Paul entered in, and prayed, and laid his hands on him, and healed him. So when this was done, others also, which had diseases in the island, came, and were healed" (Acts 28:8, 9).

The End-time prophet, Ellen G. White—"The Lord gave me great light on health reform. In connection with my husband, I was to be a medical missionary worker. I was to set an example to the church by taking the sick to my home and caring for them. This I have done, giving the women and children vigorous treatment.

"I was also to speak on the subject of Christian temperance, as the Lord's appointed messenger. I engaged heartily in this work, and spoke to large assemblies on temperance in its broadest and truest sense" (in *Review and Herald*, July 26, 1906).

Divine Origin

"True medical missionary work is of heavenly origin. It was not originated by any person who lives. But in connection with this work we see so much which dishonors God that I am instructed to say, The medical missionary work is of divine origin and has a most glorious mission to fulfill. In all its bearings it is to be in conformity with Christ's work. Those who are workers together with God will just as surely represent the character of Christ as Christ represented the character of His Father while in this world" (*Medical Ministry*, p. 24).

The Way to Reach the Unreachable

"I can see in the Lord's providences that the medical missionary work is to be a great entering wedge, whereby the diseased soul may be reached" (*Counsels on Health*, p. 535).

"God calls for thousands to work for Him, not by preaching to those who know the truth, going over and over the same ground, but by warning those who have never heard the last message of mercy. . . . Do medical missionary work. Thus you will gain access to the hearts of the people. The way will be prepared for more decided proclamation of the truth. You will find that relieving their physical suffering gives an opportunity to minister to their spiritual needs" (*A Call to Medical Evangelism and Health Education*, p. 7).

"The Lord will give you success in this work; for the gospel is the power of God unto salvation when it is interwoven with the practical life, when it is lived and practiced. The union of Christlike work for the body and Christlike work for the soul is the true interpretation of the gospel" (in *Review and Herald*, Mar. 4, 1902).

Medical Missionaries and the Cities

"Medical missionary work is the right hand of the gospel. It is necessary to the advancement of the cause of God. As through it men and women are led to see the importance of right habits of living, the saving power of the truth will be made known. Every city is to be entered by workers trained to do medical missionary work. As the right hand of the third angel's message, God's methods of treating disease will open doors for the entrance of present truth" (*Testimonies for the Church*, vol. 7, p. 59).

Plenty of Sick People, an Abundance of Work

"[All] those who do this will find a field of labor anywhere. There will be suffering ones, plenty of them, who will need help, not only among those of our own faith, but largely among those who know not the truth. The shortness of time demands an energy that has not been aroused among those who claim to believe the present truth" (*Counsels on Health*, p. 506).

The Beehive Ministry of Health

The Beehive's goal is to reestablish health reform and the gospel medical missionary program in the Seventh-day Adventist Church and the world, elevating it back to the level of importance bestowed upon the minister. It is clear, first and foremost, that was God's intent and the work of the Savior. He demonstrated that the restoration of health was just as important as the saving of souls. Unfortunately, it is also clear that currently we give little attention to this sacred function of health and healing—of pointing the sick to the loving, sympathetic Jesus. As a result, we need to emphasize the following aspects:

1. Nursing the sick.
2. Conducting seminars on healthful living and the care of the sick.
3. Building partnerships between pastors, Bible instructors, literature evangelists, and medical missionaries.
4. Anchoring health programs in city missions.
5. Reviving house-to-house labor training and the use of simple, natural remedies.
6. Establishing treatment rooms (health spas), operated as feeders to the outpost health resorts located outside of the city (such spas can share the same locality as the restaurants).
7. Establish relationships with lifestyle centers (health resorts) to help with follow-up.

The Work for Today

"Why has it not been understood from the Word of God that the work being done in medical missionary lines is a fulfillment of the scripture, 'Go out quickly into the streets and lanes of the city, and bring in hither the poor, and the maimed, and the halt, and the blind. . . . The servant said, Lord, it is done as thou hast commanded, and yet there is room. And the lord said unto the servant, Go out into the highways and hedges, and compel them to come in, that my house may be filled'" (*A Call to Medical Evangelism and Health Education*, p. 9).

"This is a work that the churches in every locality, north and south and east and west, should do. The churches have been given the opportunity of answering this work. Why have they not done it? Someone must fulfill the commission" (in *Review and Herald*, May 25, 1897).

If there is a critical reason that we must get back to medical missionary activities in the Seventh-day Adventist Church, it is that it hastens the Lord's return. Not because it wins others to Christ. It does, and it will. Consider two references, one from Scriptures and the other from the writings of Ellen G. White. First the Bible: "When the Lord shall build up Zion, he shall appear in his glory" (Ps. 102:16). Now Ellen White: "When the character of Christ shall be perfectly reproduced in His people, then He will come to claim them as His own" (*Christ's Object Lessons,* p. 69).

The character of Christ is not just some outward display. No, it is rather a heart-felt desire to help those who are sick, hurting, lost, and in darkness, just as Christ did. Notice how the next statement brings this idea home:

" 'Let us not love in word,' the apostle writes, 'but in deed and in truth.' The completeness of Christian character is attained when *the impulse to help and bless others springs constantly from within*" (*The Acts of the Apostles,* p. 551; italics supplied).

To be more like Christ, we are commissioned to do the work of Christ, that we might attain, in our own characters one like His. It explains why Christ called the twelve in Matthew 10 and endowed them with power to cast out demons and heal all manner of sickness and disease. Peter was in that group along with the disciples known as the Sons of Thunder as was Judas. They all had their respective character flaws, but Christ granted them authority. The work that Christ offers, He gives out of infinite wisdom, for it is the very thing that changes our hearts and saves us.

The Bible is clear that our deeds do not save us but rather that we work because we are saved, and in the process, we become transformed. We can never hasten the Lord's return until we, like the disciples and the early church, do the labor of Christ Himself.

The Mission in Practice . . . Words From the Front Line

Rico Hill, director, The Beehive International; author; and medical missionary, says:

"A supernatural interest in medical missionary activities has seemed to have developed lately. Many ministries have started or are developing health evangelism programs.

"Having trained multiple churches in our New Life Gospel Medical Missionary Program, we are seeing the benefits and growth of this end-time work. We have been offering weekend workshops and six-week schools, the latter also conducted primarily on the weekends. Churches have experienced revival and reformation. What has become abundantly clear is that when we study the life of Christ and recognize that He was and is the great medical missionary, people quickly see the gospel in a whole new light. Often church members during the training process say that they have never before heard the health message presented in such a way. They confess that they never knew the role that health plays in the plan of salvation. Heretofore, many have only heard the gospel message preached, but rarely how to live it. Many have not realized that Christ never separated the healing work from the proclamation of the gospel and that His life and the way in which He healed was the gospel lived out. According to *The Ministry of Healing* (p. 19), Christ did more healing than preaching. And the Bible says in 3 John 2, 'Beloved, I wish above all things that thou mayest prosper and be in health, even as thy soul prospereth.' The text tells us that it is important to God that we be just as healthy physically as we are spiritually.

"The Beehive Ministry recently conducted a six-week training program at a church in Sparks, Nevada, where we had the senior pastor, the head elder, and seven members from the church board in the gospel medical missionary class. Having them as a part of the class was a tremendous blessing. It demonstrated unity and buy-in from the leadership of the church. I believe that such a level of consensus and commitment in His church greatly pleases the Lord. Second, the congregation benefited when their church served as a training center. Most medical missionary training schools take place away from the local church—usually at some institution or independent ministry. There is nothing wrong with this model. But there can be a downside. When the one or two individuals who have been trained come back to their congregation, excited about the things they've learned, there is often very little interest, and the enthusiasm dies quickly, as would the blessing that the church and community would have received. However, when the training takes place on the grounds of the local church, it offers the greatest opportunity for spiritual renewal for the whole congregation, as there is strength in numbers. Consider this: if you have one person excited about the health message, many consider the individual as one 'health nut.' But if you have 25 to 30 people zealous about God's methods to reach the cities, you have a health team or health department.

"Finally, we saw that when the church was trained locally over six weeks, it presented to us the most effective process of studying the community, along with the students, as we assessed how best to reach their community using the health message. This doesn't work as well when individual church members, training as medical missionaries, go away to a different location to study, and then come back to the local church and attempt to implement what they've learned alone. It is not the most effective way to accomplish the true intent of the training. We have found it better to study the condition of the church and the needs of the community at the same time and then help the students first develop strategies to minister to the condition of its members and next develop plans to reach their city for Christ.

"The Beehive has now certified members across more than 20 churches, with 32 students at the Sparks SDA Church near Reno (four of whom came from California). The Lord is preparing His people to reach the cities in ways that will astound us all."

SECTION 3:
Ministry of House-to-House Labor/Gospel Workers

"He [Christ] carried His instruction into the household, bringing families in their own homes under the influence of His divine presence. His strong personal sympathy helped to win hearts" (*The Desire of Ages*, p. 151).

"By personal labor reach those around you. Become acquainted with them. Preaching will not do the work that needs to be done. Angels of God attend you to the dwellings of those you visit. This work cannot be done by proxy. Money lent or given will not accomplish it. Sermons will not do it. By visiting the people, talking, praying, sympathizing with them, you will win hearts" (*Testimonies for the Church*, vol. 9, p. 41).

Christ's Example. "The Savior went from house to house, healing the sick, comforting the mourners, soothing the afflicted, speaking peace to the disconsolate" (*The Acts of the Apostles*, p. 364).

The Call. "God is calling not only upon ministers, but also upon physicians, nurses, colporteurs, Bible workers, and other consecrated laymen of varied talent who have a knowledge of the Word of God and who know the power of His grace, to consider the needs of the unwarned cities. Time is rapidly passing, and there is much to be done. Every agency must be set in operation, that present opportunities may be wisely improved" (*ibid.*, pp. 158, 159).

The Worker. No, not the Bible instructor or literature evangelist, but the "worker" bee. God has given us yet again another wonderful object lesson in the bee itself. Let's consider it:

1. The worker bee labors harmoniously in unity.
2. The worker bee produces.
3. The worker bee remains active until the end of its life.
4. The worker bee touches many aspects of our food production.
5. What the worker bee does is essential to our very survival.

Without the worker bee, many of our crops and plants and fruit trees would not receive the pollination necessary for the growth that sustains human existence. Workers for God are critical just as is the worker bee. We have watched the varied attempts of evangelism in our church without the use of house-to-house laborers: Bible instructors, literature evangelists, and medical missionaries. Our efforts have been, and continue to be, by and large unsuccessful. The house-to-house element of our city missions is essential and should touch every aspect of urban outreach.

The Vision. "I was shown this same place at another time. I saw two Bible workers seated in a family. With the open Bibles before them, they presented the Lord Jesus Christ as the sin-pardoning Savior. Their words were spoken with freshness and power. Earnest prayer was offered to God, and hearts were softened and subdued by the softening influence of the Spirit of God. As the Word of God was explained, I saw that a soft, radiant light illuminated the Scriptures, and I said softly, 'Go out into the highways and hedges, and compel them to come in, that my house may be filled'" (*Evangelism*, p. 457).

We Must Work in Unity

"Unity in diversity is God's plan. Among the followers of Christ there is to be the blending of diverse elements, one adapted to the other, and each to do its special work for God. Every individual has his place in the filling up of one great plan bearing the stamp of Christ's image. . . . The Spirit of God, working in and through the diverse elements, will produce harmony of action. . . . There is to be only one master spirit—the Spirit of Him who is infinite in wisdom, and in whom all the diverse elements meet in beautiful, matchless unity" (Ellen G. White letter 78, 1894).

"My brethren, the Lord calls for unity, for oneness. We are to be one in the faith. I want to tell you that when the gospel ministers and the medical missionary workers are not united, there is placed on our churches the worst evil that can be placed there. Our medical missionaries ought to be interested in the work of our conferences, and our conference workers ought to be as much interested in the work of our medical missionaries" (*Medical Ministry*, p. 241).

Uniting Ministers, Bible Instructors, Literature Evangelists, and Medical Missionaries.

"Set to work the young men and the young women in our churches. Combine the medical missionary work with the proclamation of the third angel's message. Make regular, organized effort to lift the churches out of the dead level into which they have fallen and have remained for years. Send into the churches workers who will set the principles of health reform in their connection with the third angel's message before every family and individual. Encourage all to take a part in work for their fellowmen, and see if the breath of life will not quickly return to these churches" (*Testimonies to Ministers and Gospel Workers,* p. 415).

"Medical missionary work is the pioneer work of the gospel, the door through which the truth for this time is to find entrance to many homes. God's people are to be genuine medical missionaries; for they are to learn to minister to the needs of both soul and body. . . . As they go from house to house they will find access to many hearts. Many will be reached who otherwise never would have heard the gospel message" (in *Review and Herald,* Dec. 17, 1914).

"The ministerial evangelist who engages in the canvassing work is performing a service fully as important as that of preaching the gospel before a congregation Sabbath after Sabbath. God looks upon the faithful evangelistic canvasser with as much approval as He looks upon any faithful minister. Both workers have light, and both are to shine in their respective spheres of influence. God calls upon every man to cooperate with the great Medical Missionary Worker, and to go forth into the highways and byways. Each man, in his particular line of service, has a work to do for God. Such laborers, if converted, are true missionaries" (Ellen G. White letter 186, 1903).

"Begin to do medical missionary work with the conveniences which you have at hand. You will find that thus the way will open for you to hold Bible readings" (*Medical Ministry,* p. 239).

"Christ came to the earth to walk and work among the poor. To the poor He preached the gospel. His work is the gospel worked out on medical missionary lines—in justice, mercy, and the love of God which is the sure fruit borne because the tree is good. And today in the person of His believing, working children, who move under the guidance of the Holy Spirit, Christ visits the poor and the needy, relieving want and alleviating suffering"(Ellen G. White letter 83, 1902).

United with the Ministry of the Churches. "It is not the plan of God to have some eased and others burdened. Some feel the weight and responsibility of the cause, and the necessity of their acting that they may gather with Christ and not scatter abroad. Others go on free from any responsibility, acting as though they had no influence. Such scatter abroad. God is not partial. All who are made partakers of His salvation here, and who hope to share the glories of the kingdom hereafter, must gather with Christ. . . . Said the angel: 'Every talent God will require with usury.' Every Christian must go on from strength to strength, and employ all his powers in the cause of God" (*Testimonies for the Church,* vol. 1, p. 179).

God's remnant church has in so many ways lost its connection with the communities in the cities. Each congregation should have committed members who are working to lead others to Christ. Likewise, each one should have dedicated individuals visiting interested homes. Unfortunately, that is not the case. The Beehive concept, however, can revive the local congregation and existing ministries, adding to them Bible instructors, medical missionaries, and literature evangelists. By God's grace, it will restore the bridge between the church and the community and will work, in a structured way, sharing the needs and interest from people gathered in the community with the local church. Done on a consistent, ongoing basis, it will keep the church busy and functional, allowing its members to be engaged and involved in winning others for Christ. But it starts with willing hearts revived for the work of Christ and clean hands trained and equipped for service.

United With Integrated Personal and Public Evangelism. "A well-balanced work can be carried on best in the cities when a Bible school for the training of workers is in progress while public meetings are being held. Connected with this training-school or city mission should be experienced laborers of deep spiritual understanding, who can give the Bible-workers daily instruction, and who can also unite whole-heartedly in the general public effort" (*Gospel Workers,* p. 364).

The Beehive concept will encourage church members to participate with each public outreach. When someone demonstrates an ability to preach, we should call upon them to present the gospel as well as play a key role in the ongoing training of others.

Bible instructors and medical missionaries can also help out in vegetarian restaurants and serve in thrift stores and other places of business where they can draw close to the people and be channels of light for Christ. Here is ministry integration on the personal level.

United With Ministry to the Poor. Such forms of ministry, which include the visitation of the sick and shut-in, those in prison, and those who generally have no hope, should receive great emphasis. Those constantly involved in such areas will touch the lives of people with the love of Christ. More and more people need simple help whether it is food, encouragement, housing, job training, etc.

United With the Food Ministry. Whether it is distributing food from the pantry at the evangelistic center or helping out at a vegetarian restaurant or health food store, the Bible instructor will play a role in this ministry.

United With the Health Ministry. The Bible instructor who is also a medical missionary will greatly aid health ministry efforts.

United With the Outpost Health Resort. As church members labor from house to house, the needs of those they meet will especially be apparent. It will be an amazing opportunity to share the health message and point individuals to lifestyle courses, whether at a Beehive meeting in the city or at the outpost health resort in the country. In fact, the Bible instructors will be our most active ambassadors and "Christ-brand marketing experts" for the evangelistic centers, restaurants, and country health retreats.

United With Ministry to the Prisons. There is a great need for the gospel to enter the prisons. As presented in chapter 2, Christ considered it of great importance to grant a pardon to a guilty prisoner as He hung upon the cross. Just as it is critical to share the last message of warning to those in spiritual bondage, the gospel worker must not overlook sharing the three angels' messages with those physically incarcerated. As those who lead prison ministries make connections with the prison systems and arrange for literature to get into the jails, gospel workers should labor alongside this ministry. It not only offers opportunities to present health talks, distribute literature, and give Bible studies, but prisoners often share what they are learning or even the material they receive with those on the outside. They often want someone to visit their relatives. The gospel worker will follow up such contacts.

Bible Instruction, a Thorough Method. "In every city that is entered a solid foundation is to be laid for permanent work. The Lord's methods are to be followed. By doing house-to-house work, by giving Bible readings in families, the worker may gain access to many who are seeking for truth. By opening the Scriptures, by prayer, by exercising faith, he is to teach the people the way of the Lord" (*Testimonies for the Church,* vol. 7, p. 38).

The Mission in Practice . . . Words From the Front Line

Andre Waller, founder of The Mission, a missionary training school in South Lancaster, Massachusetts, and the students he teaches have an active city ministry reaching the city of Boston and surrounding suburbs. He directs a training course called Fully Integrated Restoration Evangelism (FIRE) that not only presents effective evangelism in theory, but also carries it out in reality. He comments on what he considers to be the three most important elements of twenty-first-century literature evangelism:

1. "**Have goals.** 'Success in any line demands a definite aim' (*Education,* p. 262). Before getting started, know what your goals are. Put them in writing and present them to the church first and then to God. Let the church pray over them.

2. "**Know your product.** Make sure you are living what you are selling. In other words, it is not profitable to sell books you haven't read. And, having read them, it is an offense to God to read the books and not live up to what you're selling.

3. "**Pray.** It is needed at every step of the work—prayer and more prayer."

Eugene Prewitt, Bible and church history instructor, Amazing Facts
What are the most important elements of twenty-first-century literature evangelism?

1. "**Smile.** Literature evangelists must take charge of their nonverbal communication. And the place to begin is the face. The science of smiling involves much more of the face than the lips. In fact, lip-only smiles wear the smiler out and put a fatigued expression on the rest of the face.

2. "**Know what you are going to say and be ready and comfortable with it.** We do not arrive at the door by invitation. For that reason we cannot expect that we will meet everyone at a convenient time. Many will be on their way out. Others will have food in danger of burning, or a friend on hold on the telephone.

   "In such situations, the literature evangelist should be ready to give a highly abbreviated version of the sales presentation. It will assure customers that you recognize the value and seriousness of their time constraints. They may then reciprocate that respect by slowing down and asking questions, or they may just pull out money for the book and close the door. Either way, the technique has worked.

3. "**Pray.** Some key points about prayer include that what we expect is relevant to

what will happen. We must build upon divine promises, bolstering our prayers by our energetic cooperation. Furthermore, our prayers must be constant—not ones of meaningless repetition but demonstrations of our dependence on God.

4. "**Get the book into the customer's hand.** Imagine that you are in a grocery store (I use this illustration in training) and your cart is half full. An elderly man approaches your cart, looks in, and says, 'There it is! I've been looking for that!' and proceeds to remove the box of raisins from your cart.

"How would you feel? The raisins are not yours. After all, you have not paid for them. They belong to the store, and it doesn't care who buys them. But you possess them. The fact that they are in your cart imparts a partial sense of ownership. It works the same with our books. Until your customers have them in their hands, they do not feel seriously interested. They will not pay much attention to what you say or have any desire to buy them.

"Each of the preceding points needs explaining, guidance, and practice to do well. If you eliminate any one of those four aspects, you stand a good chance of failing. Literature evangelism is highly complex, and you must keep these principles in mind if you want to do it professionally."

SECTION 4:
Ministry to the Rich:
Integrated Evangelism

"Plan to reach the best classes, and you will not fail to reach the lower classes" (Evangelism, p. 553).

In Luke 8:1-3 we see an element highly relevant to our day: "And it came to pass afterward, that he went throughout every city and village, preaching and shewing the glad tidings of the kingdom of God: and the twelve were with him, and certain women, which had been healed of evil spirits and infirmities, Mary called Magdalene, out of whom went seven devils, and Joanna the wife of Chuza Herod's steward, and Susanna, and many others, which ministered unto him of their substance."

Clearly the women had means that they used to support Jesus and His work. Notice what Jesus (and perhaps the disciples) had done for them. They had healed them of their infirmities. Notice that the next thing the Bible records is that those women gave of their substance (their money). Jesus did not wait for money to come in before He would go forward with His ministry in the cities and villages. Instead, He began the work of healing as the great medical missionary and the financial support then materialized. Of course, Jesus could have gotten money from the mouth of a fish. But this experience in Luke gives us a glimpse into the method of the Savior. And it is a formula for us today. We should not wait until we have all the money needed for all of the facets of city ministry before we get started. God has outlined the blueprint.

Now, we must understand that we don't go out to the highways and byways and minister to the physical needs of the rich so that we can receive money. Many often refer to what Christ did as disinterested benevolence. That is to say, He would have done it whether it yielded fruit or not. He came to minister and be a servant and not to be ministered to. In fact, often He knew that the lepers He healed would not even return to say thank You. But our Redeemer healed nonetheless. The financial blessings came as a natural consequence. Therefore, we are to go out and love the people with disinterested benevolence and leave the results to God.

Jesus' life shows us that He went forward in faith that God would provide for ministry needs. We see that the Lord has promised the same for us today. Let's look at how *The Ministry of Healing* presents this blueprint method from the Gospel of Luke as end-time counsel for the remnant church:

"The greatest men of the earth are not beyond the power of a wonder-working God. If those who are workers together with Him will do their duty bravely and faithfully, God will convert men who occupy responsible places, men of intellect and influence. Through the power of the Holy Spirit, many will be led to accept the divine principles.

"When it is made plain that the Lord expects them as His representatives to relieve suffering humanity, many will respond and will give of their means and their sympathies for the benefit of the poor. As their minds are thus drawn away from their own selfish interests, many will surrender themselves to Christ. With their talents of influence and means they will gladly unite in the work of beneficence with the humble missionary who was God's agent in their conversion. By a right use of their earthly treasures they will lay up for themselves 'a treasure in the heavens that faileth not, where no thief approacheth, neither moth corrupteth.'

"When converted to Christ, many will become agencies in the hand of God to work for others of their own class. They will feel that a dispensation of the gospel is committed to them for those who have made this world their all. Time and money will be consecrated to God, talent and influence will be devoted to the work of winning souls to Christ" (p. 216).

We also can consider the story of Nicodemus and Joseph of Arimathea. During Jesus' life it seemed as though the gospel message did not really affect them. The wealthy of the earth perhaps are living in fear of what their peers may think of them if caught listening to such a message as that of the three angels. But the reality was that one night a private encounter with Jesus converted Nicodemus.

Imagine how Christ rejoiced to see that His meeting with Nicodemus had not been in vain. In heaven we will experience the same rejoicing when we see how many of the rich among us were converted because we ministered to their physical health.

We have a message that is for the high and low, the rich and poor. It is time to get serious about how strategically to reach the rich of our world. They are ready to respond. Many of our nation's most affluent have lost their wealth during the past few years. Maybe soon it will all be gone. We can encourage them that their life of hard work has not been in vain. They can join us and use their means to spread the news to the world that Christ is soon to return.

Here is one example of what someone from the Beehive has done recently.

The opportunity arose to speak to a large crowd of wealthy Americans that had retired in a resort area. Flyers invited them to a seminar dubbed "How to Thrive in the Coming Economic Downturn." Many Jews, Catholics, "unchurched," and others showed up. The event was free of charge. The three-night seminar simply sought to answer three questions: What is happening in the world economy? Who is really behind it? How can we thrive going forward?

The first topic covered was the economy's role in prophecy, i.e., the coming period when no one will be able to buy or sell without permission. The next concerned the role of the little horn and its desire to gain control of the world. Last, the third night dealt with preparation by applying principles that Seventh-day Adventists have for a long time perhaps taken for granted, such as growing your own food and living outside the major metropolitan areas and starting your own business.

It may sound as if the seminar presented too much information in just three nights. However, the results were amazing. People requested more studies, and such meetings have been repeated in many places. Do not for a second believe that the rich will not listen to the three angels' messages. Ellen G. White tells us that we are to make the messages attractive. We are to accomplish this by illustrating the gospel through medical missionary work. When we have shown the gospel, not by words, but by a loving heart that will relieve the suffering of the sick, the rich and poor will see love in the three angels' messages.

Notice the following pointed statement:

"That which will reach them [the rich] effectually is a consistent, unselfish presentation of the gospel of Christ" (*The Ministry of Healing,* p. 213).

Here we find the very heart of how we are to minster to the rich. It must be an *"unselfish presentation of the gospel."* We have been demonstrating how synergistic opportunities exist between the various ministries within the Beehive structure. Genuine medical missionary work, we have learned, is the gospel practiced or illustrated. If the gospel is to display itself in all its glory, we must present it unselfishly. What does this mean? Does it involve never holding back a conversation or Bible study? Certainly that is part of it. But to reach the cities, we must reveal the gospel not through words but through an unselfish life that lives out its principles. The rich will need to see them. With skeptics and secularists existing, by and large, among the wealthiest of our nation, it is they who must witness Christianity manifested in daily experience. But how will that happen?

Let us consider a few ways that will attract their attention to such a demonstration of the gospel. Those living lavishly on rich foods and the standard American diet will often be the sickest among us. The rich, who often tend to be intemperate in all things, will require the assistance of those willing to spend nights at their bedside helping to restore their health and vitality when the doctors send them home to die. Here is one of the greatest presentations of the gospel.

Paul powerfully corroborates this idea in 1 Corinthians 2:1-5: "I, brethren, when I came to you, came not with excellency of speech or of wisdom, declaring unto you the testimony of God. For I determined not to know any thing among you, save Jesus Christ, and him crucified. . . . My speech and my preaching was not with enticing words of man's wisdom, but in demonstration of the Spirit and of power: that your faith should not stand in the wisdom of men, but in the power of God."

In order that we might reach the rich, we must minister with the "demonstration of the Spirit and of power." The whole world, including the wealthy, will witness the great power of the gospel in God's people when they are willing do whatever is necessary to reach the fallen.

Another powerful way in which we can influence them is through seeking to become part of their daily lives. What would that look like? Ellen White's statement gives us one idea:

"Our workers should present before these men [the wealthy] a plain statement of our plan of labor, telling them what we need in order to help the poor and needy and to establish this work on a firm basis. Some of these will be impressed by the Holy Spirit to invest the Lord's means in a way that will advance His cause. They will fulfill His purpose by helping to create centers of influence in the large cities. Interested workers will be led to offer themselves for various lines of missionary effort. Hygienic restaurants will be established. But with what carefulness should this work be done!" (*Testimonies for the Church,* vol. 7, p. 112).

Imagine the relationships that will result from daily interaction with those who patronize our restaurants in the cities. "I have been instructed that one of the principal reasons why hygienic restaurants and treatment rooms should be established in the centers of large cities is that by this means the attention of leading men will be called to the third angel's message" (*ibid.,* pp. 122, 123).

Based on the way we conduct ourselves, the superiority of our food, and in light of the fact that we are closed on Sabbath, many will ask us why we do what we do. It will give us the opportunity to share at the appropriate time what it is that motivates us.

Another story from Scripture is that of Cornelius. It shows us the fruit of going after those outside of our faith who hold positions of influence.

"Cornelius, the Roman centurion, was a man of wealth and of noble birth. His position was one of trust and honor. A heathen by birth, training, and education, through contact with the Jews he had gained a knowledge of the true God, and he worshiped Him, showing the sincerity of his faith by compassion to the poor. He gave 'alms to the people, and prayed to God alway.' Acts 10:2, ARV. . . .

"So today God is seeking for souls among the high as well as the low. There are many like Cornelius, men whom He desires to connect with His church" (*The Ministry of Healing,* p. 209).

Sadly, it is much easier to have a fund-raising campaign to build an orphanage or homeless shelter or even a soup kitchen than it is to raise money to start a restaurant located in the wealthiest part of the city.

Think of these men and women who are working tireless hours in the rat race, yet who is ministering to them? Do we not think that the hope of heaven would be an inspiration to them just as much as it is to those begging for bread?

"He that loveth silver shall not be satisfied with silver; nor he that loveth abundance with increase" (Eccl. 5:10). "If I have said to fine gold, Thou art my confidence, . . . I should have denied the God that is above" (Job 31:24-28). "None of them can by any means redeem his brother, nor give to God a ransom for him: (For the redemption of their soul is precious, and it ceaseth forever)" (Ps. 49:7, 8).

All the money in the world will not satisfy the longing of the heart. The rich, just like the poor, are looking for something that will fill the empty void that the wealth of our world cannot. They know that there is something out there that brings joy and happiness, but they have not been able to find it yet.

"Few among them go to church; for they feel that they receive little benefit. The teaching they hear does not touch the heart. Shall we make no personal appeal to them?" (*The Ministry of Healing*, p. 210).

Many wealthy men and women are drowning out their miserable lives with alcohol, drugs, affairs, gambling, or any number of vices that clearly reveal them as unhappy and dissatisfied no matter how deeply they delve into such behaviors. Such individuals clearly have talents, and if used for the kingdom of heaven as did Cornelius or Nicodemus, imagine what could take place today?

"Some are especially fitted to work for the higher classes. These should seek wisdom from God to know how to reach these persons, to have not merely a casual acquaintance with them, but by personal effort and living faith to awaken them to the needs of the soul, to lead them to a knowledge of the truth as it is in Jesus" (*ibid.*, p. 213).

We should not think for a moment that in order to reach the rich we have to eat what they eat or dress like they dress or drive what they drive. That is just playing the same meaningless game that imprisons them. We are to show them a better way completely different than what they currently are experiencing.

"The greatest men of the earth are not beyond the power of a wonder-working God. If those who are workers together with Him will do their duty bravely and faithfully, God will convert men who occupy responsible places, men of intellect and influence. Through the power of the Holy Spirit, many will be led to accept the divine principles" (*ibid.*, p. 216).

The Mission in Practice . . . Words From the Front Line

Jared Thurmon, director, The Beehive International, on Ministering to the Rich—A Personal Experience With the Role of Restaurants in the Cities:

"A few months back as some friends and I were studying the role of restaurants in evangelism, we began to dream about where the ideal spot in the world would be to start one. As we discussed the big cities of the world where thought leaders work we realized that one exceeds them all: New York City. To be even more specific, we zeroed in on Wall Street.

"If you think about it, there is not a more influential place on earth. What happens there, affects the entire world. The global economy is tied in essence to the U.S dollar. From the price of oil to that of gold, all is valued in comparison to U.S. dollars.

"So having said that, I endeavored to understand more of the history of Adventists in New York City. Had we started restaurants before? Were they successful? Were there any still in operation?

"With all of those questions in my mind, I began my search. I eventually found a place located on Wall Street run by a Seventh-day Adventist. The mission of this restaurant was to fulfill their calling as outlined in the writings of Ellen G. White.

"I booked my flight and headed to New York City, where I spent three days digesting this new-to-me concept—an Adventist-run, mission-based restaurant. I witnessed with my own eyes and interacted with some of the most influential people on the earth. I heard executives telling me how much they valued this restaurant. I listened as they explained how they had lost weight, lowered their cholesterol, etc. just by finding this restaurant, and they were starting to implement some of the ideas that the restaurant and its staff encouraged. The place offered cooking classes twice a month, and people attended them to learn more about the innovative lifestyle principles they shared.

"The printed material the restaurant left lying around seemed to be nonintrusive, and I can say that I saw the reason God has called us to do restaurants in the largest cities."

SECTION 5:
Ministry to the Poor:
Integrated Evangelism

It is clear that Jesus had a special place in His heart for the poor. Our merciful, all-powerful Savior could eradicate poverty in an instance, yet He said, "For the poor always ye have with you; but me ye have not always" (John 12:8).

God leaves the poor among us so that we might minister to them, while at the same time cure our own sin of selfishness.

"Constant, self-denying benevolence is God's remedy for the cankering sins of selfishness and covetousness. God has arranged systematic benevolence to sustain His cause and relieve the necessities of the suffering and needy. He has ordained that giving should become a habit, that it may counteract the dangerous and deceitful sin of covetousness. Continual giving starves covetousness to death" (*The Adventist Home*, p. 370).

God designed a way for us to minister to those in need, and that at the same time transforms our own characters. But that's not all. Jesus wants us to care for the poor, and when we do, it is like giving Him a loan. Yes, the Sovereign of the universe allows sinful humanity to make Him a debtor and to be held accountable for repaying the debt. While it almost sounds blasphemous, Scripture declares: "He that hath pity upon the poor lendeth unto the Lord; and that which he hath given will he pay him again" (Prov. 19:17).

If we would just begin to work among the poor as the Bible has commissioned us to, how soon would we see thousands won to Christ? We must take up Christ's mission. Many times that mission might be just praying with those who are broken and discouraged.

"The mission of Christ was to heal the sick, encourage the hopeless, and bind up the brokenhearted. This work of restoration is to be carried on among the needy, suffering ones of humanity. God calls not only for your benevolence, but your cheerful countenance, your hopeful words, the grasp of your hand. Relieve some of God's afflicted ones. Some are sick, and hope has departed. Bring back the sunlight to them. There are souls who have lost their courage;

speak to them, pray for them. There are those who need the bread of life. Read to them from the Word of God. There is a soul sickness no balm can reach, no medicine heal. Pray for these, and bring them to Jesus Christ. And in all your work, Christ will be present to make impressions upon human hearts" (*A Call to Medical Evangelism and Health Education*, p. 23).

We are to be involved in:

(1) visiting the sick and destitute

(2) visiting shut-ins/prisons, etc. (as counseled by Christ)

(3) the distribution of food/clothing (as counseled by Christ)

(4) homeless ministry/a comprehensive approach to help people get "back on track"

(5) having rehabilitation resource information available for those requiring it (a critical urban street need)

Each city should have leaders who will coordinate visitations to the sick and those in prisons. Assistance should be given to those who cannot help themselves. It could include miscellaneous housework, and/or yard work, grocery buying, running essential errands, and distributing food and clothing.

Working With Single Parents/Widows/Foster Children/Adoptions

This is most valuable in aiding the fatherless in finding a family that will love and care for them. Working with local adoption agencies and then keeping in touch and spending time with the youth is our duty. Other vital activities include:

(1) finding work for the unemployed

(2) finding housing for the working class

(3) teaching trades/personal skills/business start-up techniques

(4) teaching men how to be servant leaders in their homes

(5) teaching men how to be excellent fathers and fiscally responsible

The mission of helping the unemployed and educating men is at the heart of the Bible and the gospel commission. Such a program should involve many aspects. It would include training classes in all aspects of life and should seek to involve as many church members as possible in fulfilling the task. We should teach classes—from cooking to gardening to public speaking to computer skills. Furthermore, we propose to help each person in finding work and assist them in any way possible. In addition, we would suggest that your church look up local homeless shelters in your city and consider volunteering to provide a Sabbath lunch once a month. Offer to do health seminars there. Perhaps your church can open a food pantry so that the community knows you have food for those in need. Start a clothing drive and have items on hand for families that have hit hard times. Collect a special offering once per month for the impoverished and homeless.

A church-Beehive partnership, with the bringing together of diverse talents and backgrounds, can ensure that its goals are systematically fulfilled.

Ministering to the Wealthy and the Poor at the Same Time

Countless men and women have all the means and goods this life can offer and yet are dying for what only Christ can provide. We can seek out the wealthy and share the gospel, which will give them "peace that passeth all understanding." Programs on better health, both physically and spiritually, will attract all classes.

Statistics now show that the wealthy currently comprise one of the fastest growing demographics of those adopting a healthy lifestyle and in particular a plant-based diet. And as we have already seen in the writings of Ellen G. White, when we seek the wealthy, we will also reach the poor.

SECTION 6:
Ministry of Food Science:
Integrated Evangelism

Why did Jesus heal more than He preached? Why should we promote health more than traditional evangelistic preaching today?

As we have repeatedly seen, the answer is medical missionary work.

Please don't think that we are proposing to exalt the health ministry above the gospel ministry. Promoting health is the right arm and the gospel ministry is the body. Christ healed more because He understood that the right arm opened the door.

You do not have to be a physician to participate. To reiterate the truth of the matter, the term that Adventists commonly used many years ago was *benevolent work*. Eventually *medical missionary* activity became the more popular term. Think of doing good constantly for your fellow human beings because love springs out of your heart. This is true medical missionary work, and it goes hand in hand with the gospel as described in Matthew 25 and Isaiah 58.

"Medical missionary work is the right hand of the gospel. It is necessary to the advancement of the cause of God. As through it men and women are led to see the importance of right habits of living, the saving power of the truth will be made known. Every city is to be entered by workers trained to do medical missionary work. As the right hand of the third angel's message, God's methods of treating disease will open doors for the entrance of present truth. Health literature must be circulated in many lands. Our physicians in Europe and other countries should awake to the necessity of having health works prepared by men who are on the ground and who can meet the people where they are with the most essential instruction" (*Testimonies for the Church*, vol. 7, p. 59).

How important is a hand? Think of trying to open a door with your mouth. It just does not get the job done as easy. Now, we can say that it is possible that preaching can get some people's attention, but we can reach the majority only by first entering into their lives with something they desire or need. More often than not it relates in some way with their health or that of a loved one.

"We have come to a time when every member of the church should take hold of medical missionary work. The world is a lazar house filled with victims of both physical and spiritual disease. Everywhere people are perishing for lack of a knowledge of the truths that have been committed to us. The members of the church are in need of an awakening, that they may realize their responsibility to impart these truths. Those who have been enlightened by the truth are to be light bearers to the world. To hide our light at this time is to make a terrible mistake. The message to God's people today is: 'Arise, shine; for thy light is come, and the glory of the Lord is risen upon thee'" (*ibid.*, p. 62).

Ellen White wrote that statement more than 100 years ago. If the time had come then, what do we say about today? For some the terminology may have given the method a bad taste in people's mouths. The devil would have it so. But the truth is that despite any past unfortunate stereotypes, the time has most definitely come to take the message of health to the cities of the world so that we may find an entrance for the gospel of Christ.

Medical Missionary Approach Endorsed by Jesus

"Shall we not do all in our power to advance the work in all of our large cities? Thousands upon thousands who live near us need help in various ways. Let the ministers of the gospel remember that the Lord Jesus Christ said to His disciples: 'Ye are the light of the world. A city that is set on a hill cannot be hid.' 'Ye are the salt of the earth: but if the salt have lost his savor, wherewith shall it be salted?' Matthew 5:14, 13.

"The Lord Jesus will work miracles for His people. In the sixteenth of Mark we read: 'So then after the Lord had spoken unto them, He was received up into heaven, and sat on the right hand of God. And they went forth, and preached everywhere, the Lord working with them, and confirming the word with signs following.' Verses 19, 20. Here we are assured that the Lord was qualifying His chosen servants to take up medical missionary work after His ascension" (*ibid.*, p. 114).

How Do We Use Health Today?

With the recent research of T. Colin Campbell and the China Study and documentaries such as *Forks Over Knives,* millions are now seeing a direct link between cancer and animal products. We will examine some quotes as to why that is and what we can do to share what we know. If Seventh-day Adventists want to remain on the forefront of health education and health reform, a plant-based diet is a foundational piece.

"Let the diet reform be progressive. Let the people be taught how to prepare food without the use of milk or butter. Tell them that the time will soon come when there will be no safety in using eggs, milk, cream, or butter, because disease in animals is increasing in proportion to the increase of wickedness among men. The time is near when, because of the iniquity of the fallen race, the whole animal creation will groan under the diseases that curse our earth" (*ibid.*, p. 135).

Disease: The Cause, Prevention, and Cure

If your local hospital had a five-day waiting list to see the doctor, what would you do? Now imagine that you had a three-month waiting list. Do you know that in some countries this very issue is becoming a reality? Consider what you would do if there was some pandemic flu outbreak. The point is that we as Seventh-day Adventists should be a part of the solution in society and not any current or future problem. Notice how the following quotes say it best:

"Those who teach the principles of health reform should be intelligent in regard to disease and its causes, understanding that every action of the human agent should be in perfect harmony with the laws of life. The light God has given on health reform is for our salvation and the salvation of the world. Men and women should be informed in regard to the human habitation, fitted up by our Creator as His dwelling place, and over which He desires us to be faithful stewards. 'For ye are the temple of the living God; as God hath said, I will dwell in them, and walk in them; and I will be their God, and they shall be My people.' 2 Corinthians 6:16" (*ibid.*, p. 136).

"Hold up the principles of health reform, and let the Lord lead the honest in heart. Present the principles of temperance in their most attractive form. Circulate the books that give instruction in regard to healthful living" (*ibid.*).

New York and Other Large Cities

Though we see crime and evil increasing around the world, we do not need to give up on those living in the cities that have never heard the true gospel. We have promises that should compel us to go forward:

"There are in them [large cities] many honest souls, who, as they listen to the startling truths of the advent message, will feel the conviction of the Spirit. New York is ready to be worked. In that great city the message of truth will be given with the power of God. The Lord calls for workmen. He calls upon those who have gained an experience in the cause to take up and carry forward in His fear the work to be done in New York and in other large cities of America. He calls also for means to be used in this work" (*ibid.*, p. 55).

Think Bigger. Let's not assume that if we establish a restaurant in a city that we have achieved success. We have been counseled to open many restaurants in each city. Nor should we limit ourselves to just restaurants. Think of the resorts of the world that have so many coming to them for health rejuvenation, then consider the following statement:

"When in Los Angeles I was instructed that not only in various sections of that city, but in San Diego and in other tourist resorts of Southern California, health restaurants and treatment rooms should be established. Our efforts in these lines should include the great seaside resorts. As the voice of John the Baptist was heard in the wilderness, 'Prepare ye the way of the Lord,' so must the voice of the Lord's messengers be heard in the great tourist and seaside resorts" (*ibid.*, pp. 55, 56).

Restaurants. As we see the emphasis Ellen G. White put on the ministry potential of restaurants, it seems as if they should be the ultimate training ground. Customers are not just to notice that the food is healthy and tastes good. There should be more to the restaurant than just food.

"Every hygienic restaurant should be a school. The workers connected with it should be constantly studying and experimenting, that they may make improvement in the preparation of healthful foods. In the cities this work of instruction may be carried forward on a much larger scale than in smaller places. But in every place where there is a church, instruction should be given in regard to the preparation of simple, healthful foods for the use of those who wish to live in accordance with the principles of health reform. And the church members should impart to the people of their neighborhood the light they receive on this subject" (*ibid.*, pp. 112, 113).

"Hygienic restaurants are to be established in the cities, and by them the message of temperance is to be proclaimed. Arrangements should be made to hold meetings in connection with our restaurants. Whenever possible, let a room be provided where the patrons can be invited to lectures on the science of health and Christian temperance, where they can receive instruction on the preparation of wholesome food and on other important subjects. In these meetings there should be prayer and singing and talks, not only on health and temperance topics, but also on other appropriate Bible subjects. As the people are taught how to preserve physical health, many opportunities will be found to sow the seeds of the gospel of the kingdom" (*ibid.*, p. 115).

When people come to our restaurants they should see some literature placed around that is inviting and not overbearing. Remember, we are to build a friendship before we share with them the most distinct points of our faith. The material should be primarily on health, but it would also be beneficial to have material on spiritual principles and lessons that Christ would want them to learn.

"The burden of supplying this reading matter should be shared by all our people. All who come should be given something to read. It may be that many will leave the tract unread, but some among those in whose hands you place it may be searching for light. They will read and study what you give them, and then pass it on to others" (*ibid.*, p. 116).

The staff in our restaurants should live in such close connection with God that they would recognize the promptings of His Spirit to talk personally about spiritual things to particular individuals who come to the restaurant. This will be the combining of the medical missionary work with the proclamation of the three angels' messages, as stated in *Testimonies to Ministers and Gospel Workers*, page 415. As patrons feel the love from the staff, they will see love in the message of the third angel.

One would wonder why Ellen White would give such detailed counsel regarding restaurants if God did not desire them to be a part of the final evangelistic thrust. From the staff to even the management of the restaurant itself, the counsel is appropriate and deeply spiritual.

Management Team Principles. "With every restaurant there should be connected a man and his wife who can act as guardians of the helpers, a man and woman who love the Saviour and the souls for whom He died, and who keep the way of the Lord" (*Testimonies for the Church*, vol. 7, pp. 118. 119).

The Witness of Sabbath Observance. "A scene passed before me. I was in our restaurant in San Francisco. It was Friday. Several of the workers were busily engaged in putting up packages of such foods as could be easily carried by the people to their homes, and a number were waiting to receive these packages. I asked the meaning of this, and the workers told me that some among their patrons were troubled because, on account of the closing of the restaurant, they could not on the Sabbath obtain food of the same kind as that which they used during the week. Realizing the value of the wholesome foods obtained at the restaurant, they protested against being denied them on the seventh day and pleaded with those in charge of the restaurant to keep it open every day in the week, pointing out what they would suffer if this were not done. 'What you see today,' said the workers, 'is our answer to this demand for the health foods upon the Sabbath. These people take on Friday food that lasts over the Sabbath, and in this way we avoid condemnation for refusing to open the restaurant on the Sabbath'" (*ibid.*, pp. 121, 122).

By closing our restaurants on the Sabbath, we will witness that we value the principles of the law of God more than mere riches. As the world prepares to face the final crisis over God's law, our restaurants may be a seed that was planted in many minds.

Beehive Restaurant Application: "In San Francisco a hygienic restaurant has been opened, also a food store and treatment rooms. These are doing a good work, but their influence should be greatly extended. Other restaurants similar to the one on Market Street should be opened in San Francisco and in Oakland" (*ibid.*, p. 110).

Restaurants are not just for church members and should be located widely in large cities. They will contact many people that the pulpit or our public evangelism meetings would never reach.

Restaurants and Food Manufacturing Are Endorsed by Heaven. "From the record of the Lord's miracles in providing wine at the wedding feast and in feeding the multitude, we may learn a lesson of the highest importance. The health food business is one of the Lord's own instrumentalities to supply a necessity. The heavenly Provider of all foods will not leave His people in ignorance in regard to the preparation of the best foods for all times and occasions" (*ibid.*, p. 114).

Many will want to open a restaurant. Here are a few principles that they should keep in mind as they explore the ministry of a restaurant.

- Smaller and more locations are better than a few large restaurants.
- As often as possible, teach classes on such topics as cooking, health, and disease.
- The mission is to lead to Christ, not just make healthy sinners.
- Food should vary with the seasons with as many as possible coming from outpost health resorts.
- Use simple foods grown locally and organically if possible.
- All staff should be united on the overall mission.
- Each restaurant should function like a franchise and will follow guidelines set forth from a coordinating body.
- Have health food sales/book sales on-site.
- Serve breakfast and lunch with health classes in evenings.
- Follow a basic menu that can be adaptable globally, consisting of vegetables, fresh salads, soups, vegan desserts, fresh breads, and smoothies.
- Health tracts should be prominent.
- Decor should be attractive yet simple.
- Rent locations instead of owning them.

Objective. Although management must exercise every effort to operate the restaurant successfully, the goal must always be evangelism. Profit is not the end goal—bringing people to Christ is.

Cooking Schools. As we have seen throughout this manual, the key to a successful medical missionary program is not only helping people with their current need, but also educating them in a way so that they may in turn help others. One of the greatest ways we can do this in the field of health and nutrition is cooking schools.

"Cooking schools, conducted by wise instructors, are to be held in America and in other lands. Everything that we can do should be done to show the people the value of the reform diet" (*ibid.,* p. 126).

"Cooking schools are to be established in many places. This work may begin in a humble way, but as intelligent cooks do their best to enlighten others, the Lord will give them skill and understanding. The word of the Lord is: 'Forbid them not, for I will reveal Myself to them as their Instructor.' He will work with those who carry out His plans, teaching the people how to bring about reformation in their diet by the preparation of healthful, inexpensive foods. Thus the poor will be encouraged to adopt the principles of health reform; they will be helped to become industrious and self-reliant" (*ibid.,* p. 113).

Wherever we preach and teach, we should offer cooking schools so that both rich and poor may apply their principles into their daily lives.

"From the beginning of the health reform work, we have found it necessary to educate, educate, educate. God desires us to continue this work of educating the people. We are not to neglect it because of the effect we may fear it will have on the sales of the health foods prepared in our factories. That is not the most important matter. Our work is to show the people how they can obtain and prepare the most wholesome food, how they can cooperate with God in restoring His moral image in themselves" (*ibid.,* p. 132).

"Wherever medical missionary work is carried on in our large cities, cooking schools should be held; and wherever a strong educational missionary work is in progress, a hygienic restaurant of some sort should be established, which shall give a practical illustration of the proper selection and the healthful preparation of foods" (*ibid.,* p. 55).

Health Food Manufacturing. Much has been written about health food manufacturing, but the most practical way to put it is that God has entrusted His people with an understanding of the effects of flesh food on the human body. We can see clearly that before the Flood when they adhered to a plant-based diet, humans lived close to 1,000 years before tasting death. After the Flood, when humanity began to subscribe to a kosher diet with animal products, the life span in just a few generations began to drop by nearly 90 percent. We must remember that God created the human body to live forever.

"From the record of the Lord's miracles in providing wine at the wedding feast and in feeding the multitude, we may learn a lesson of the highest importance. The health food business is one of the Lord's own instrumentalities to supply a necessity. The heavenly Provider of all foods will not leave His people in ignorance in regard to the preparation of the best foods for all times and occasions" (*ibid.,* p. 114).

"The knowledge of methods for the manufacture of health foods, which God gave to His people as a means of helping to sustain His cause . . ." *(ibid.,* p. 129).

"Let centers of influence be made in many of the Southern cities by the opening of food stores and vegetarian restaurants. Let there also be facilities for the manufacture of simple, inexpensive health foods" *(ibid.,* p. 56).

Today, the health food business is primed and ready for another revolution just like it was at the beginning of the twentieth century with the rise of the Kellogg brand. God will give each of us wisdom to make recipes and also the ability to grow food at a much more productive rate than the norm.

"The products of each locality are to be studied and carefully investigated, to see if they cannot be combined in such a way as to simplify the production of foods and lessen the cost of manufacture and transportation. Let all do their best under the Lord's supervision to accomplish this. There are many expensive articles of food that the genius of man can combine; and yet there is no real need of using the most expensive preparations" (*Health Food Ministry,* p. 54).

"The Lord has instructed me to say that He has not confined to a few persons all the light there is to be received in regard to the best preparations of health foods. He will give to many minds in different places tact and skill that will enable them to prepare health foods suitable for the countries in which they live" (*Testimonies for the Church,* vol. 7, p. 128).

It is our duty and privilege to be a part of this revolution. Local co-ops and grocers such as Whole Foods are already in the business of buying locally grown produce and locally manufactured products. Explore the opportunities in your area and believe that God will give the increase.

We find examples of this even now by Seventh-day Adventists around North America, such as Silver Hills Bakery, Heritage Health Foods, and WayFare Foods.

For a fuller and more comprehensive view of the health food manufacturing ministry, we encourage you to read the small booklet entitled *Health Food Ministry,* by Ellen G. White.

The Mission in Practice . . . Words From the Front Line—Health

Food Manufacturing

Don Otis, founder, Heritage Health Food

Why did you get into health food manufacturing?

"I had no idea that I would ever be in the health food business. However, after 20 years in the publishing program, I had an opportunity to take a position with Worthington Foods. I saw firsthand that the food and health message was a vital part of the daily lifestyle and well-being of church members, and that if you did well marketing and selling food, you could not only provide assistance to the needs of the church and others, but also help financially support the spreading of the gospel commission. I felt then, and as I look back now, the direct leading of the Lord in my life to move to a life of health food!"

What are the three most important principles to be successful in health food manufacturing?

"Let the Lord lead in all things.

"Follow the bounty of wisdom given us as a church.

"Run your business with a professional quality second to none as you represent the Lord in the marketplace."

What would you tell anyone looking to see how health food manufacturing is a ministry?

"This is a question that I could write a book on! Simply stated, I believe that when God was giving direction at the beginning of the SDA Church, He also led others to start the health food business. It was His plan that His people needed to be healthy and must eat a simple diet in order to withstand the test of evil and to have clear minds as in the days of Daniel. Also, more than just His chosen people, the world also needs what He revealed to us. Presenting it should be our constant responsibility and vision. Both His church and the world must have health foods. He entrusted us with this mission.

"Also, sharing Christ and His gospel in the marketplace on a daily basis leads to unlimited contacts in all aspects of food manufacturing. It opens many, many sharing opportunities!"

What is the most difficult aspect to health food manufacturing?

"I would have to say that the wide spectrum of beliefs in what is considered healthy and what is not is a difficult one, and many do not fully understand the clear principles that God gave us. I tried for years to make changes from within large corporate food manufacturers, but the overall unified vision for the best, most healthful food we could make was not consistently voiced by consumers, undercutting any attempt to raise the standards. It is very disappointing that many outside of the church desired higher-quality foods than we had become used to. In many ways, we have been left behind in this country by those in health food manufacturing. Now it is time to change that, and that continues to be my goal."

What advice would you give to a fellow Seventh-day Adventist seeking to get involved in health food manufacturing?

"Pray earnestly about what you can do to fit into the Lord's plan for you and how He can use you to assist in this mighty ministry!"

Kelly Coffin, WayFare Foods

Why did you get involved in food manufacturing?

"For one reason, and one reason alone. After I read the *Testimonies*, it was very clear we were to do this work. I saw that we were to become an active, daily presence in people's lives through our business practices. I saw a great need of the formation of industry and a physical, eye-to-eye presence for our people to begin reaching the people in the cities."

Why did you start with dairy products?

"I was raised on a dairy farm. I came from a line of dairy farmers in Vermont. When I became a Seventh-day Adventist and read about the dangers of dairy, the truth hit me square in the face. I saw that God had promised He would give us products from the earth that would replace meat and dairy. Dairy was what I knew. Dairy is typically the most difficult to give up when removing animal products from the diet. I learned how the consumption of dairy leads to an increase in the desire for stronger tasting animal products, such as meat, etc. Many don't understand that dairy is addictive and, as we see today, also leads to a whole host of preventable lifestyle-related diseases such as the ones the China Study entails.

"We immediately saw an improvement in our family's health when we removed dairy from our diet."

What is the most difficult aspect to health food manufacturing?

"The most difficult aspect is having faith in God's Word and pushing ahead with righteous principles. It is very tempting to begin using ingredients that are cheaper and unhealthy.

"The first step is the hard part. You have to go forward before you can see any signs. The signs will follow."

What advice would you give someone interested in food manufacturing?

"First, believe in the Lord and His promises. Believe what He has told you and don't second-guess His leading.

"Second, start in your kitchen with your family. Let your employees, friends, coworkers, and neighbors try everything you are creating. Always keep the mission, industry, the larger picture, simplicity, and duplicity in mind as you create your food.

"Never create any food without getting on your knees in your kitchen and asking for wisdom from the One who has told us to do this very special work. Also, get your children involved with you if possible."

The Mission in Practice . . . Words From the Front Line— Cooking Schools

Samantha Edwards, codirector, Tree of Life Ministries

How do you see a cooking class as a ministry?

"Cooking classes afford the opportunity to reach many classes of people in one, non-intimidating setting. Because so many people are interested in how they can create healthier meals for their families, they are more receptive. It is here that the cooking instructor can gain an entrance to spread the truth not only about the physical advantages of a plant-based diet, but more important, the spiritual benefits gained through eating in such a manner—to have a clear mind to hear the Holy Spirit's voice. This is the great object of ministering through a cooking class."

What are the three most important details to have a successful cooking class?

1. "**Plan ahead!** Have a set menu and ensure that you have all ingredients, supplies, and tools available (i.e., blenders, pots, utensils, etc.). Don't depend on anyone to bring ingredients essential for the class. What they have may not be what you're looking for, and they may show up late. Make sure that the meals are precooked just in case there are any mishaps during the class. Also, prepare enough food for sampling—people love to eat!
2. "**Keep it exciting!** If you are energetic and sound as if you believe what you're talking about, it will naturally rub off on others and encourage them to make the necessary changes in their own life.
3. "**Keep the focus on Christ!** Pray before, during, and after the cooking class."

What do you find is the most difficult thing about a cooking class?

"**The preparation leading up to it.** Usually my cooking classes are on a Sunday, so that means late Saturday, after sunset, I'm up preparing and ensuring that most of the dishes are made. Then I'm up early on Sunday morning before the class, seeing that everything is just right. If I am doing four dishes, I like to have four trays set up with each recipe already premeasured. It ensures for smooth, seamless transitions."

Do you have any other advice for someone wanting to start doing cooking classes?

"**Pray and ask God to lead you.** Make certain that you familiarize yourself with each ingredient, why it is used, and what benefit it has on the body. For instance, say I'm making almond milk, I'll talk about the fact that almonds are rich in calcium and help to regulate blood pressure."

From the Mission Field . . . in Their Own Words— Restaurants and Food Service

Seventh-day Adventists are involved with many things. We have a number of lifestyle centers around the United States, have the largest Protestant education system in the world, and operate hundreds of hospitals around the globe. Adventists have a reputation for doing pretty well at these things.

But Ellen White talks quite a bit about one thing that we don't seem to do as well: running restaurants. No one can quite put their finger on it, but for some reason we don't succeed in the majority of attempts at managing restaurants in the cities.

There is something unique about a restaurant in that church members go into the city and plant themselves among people who know nothing of the gospel. By doing this we have opportunity to connect with them on a personal level and to show that we desire their good. It is one of the best avenues to build a relationship with someone. Think of the businesses you frequent on a weekly basis because you enjoy their food or like the people who are working there.

In light of this, we sought out Adventists experienced in managing restaurants or who had been involved in food service. What are the secrets they have discovered? How can we learn from their experiences? At the same time, we interviewed secular fast-food restaurant managers and owners to find out what made their endeavors successful. One comment we got from an Adventist was that the majority of our ventures in restaurants are underfunded from the beginning. We are too shortsighted, it seems. Restaurants typically make the majority of their profits from alcohol or on the weekends. Both of these practices are not possible in an Adventist restaurant. While God has called us to operate restaurants, we must approach them with caution.

We heard a common theme from the people we asked about the secret to excellent food service. Scripture sums it up: "And out of the ground made the Lord God to grow every tree that is pleasant to the sight, and good for food; the tree of life also in the midst of the garden, and the tree of knowledge of good and evil" (Gen. 2:9).

Notice the order of the statements above. The first characteristic is that it is "pleasant" to the eyes, or in other words, it is appealing. The second is also important but just after appearance, and that is the taste of the food itself.

We had the opportunity to find out the best practices and information from a number of Adventist-run restaurants as well as some of the nation's top fast-food chains. Among the latter, we interviewed franchisees and owners of establishments such as Subway, Chipotle, Zaxby's, Panera, Freshii, Smashburger, Wok Stars, Which Wich, and more. In this manual we have focused primarily on what we found among Adventist-run restaurants, though in a few instances summarized all those whom we interviewed.

The following are experiences from Adventist-owned restaurants and one involved in high-end food service.

d'Sozo—an Adventist-run restaurant in Wichita, Kansas

Nature's Bounty—located in one of the poorest counties in California

Scott Beckett—in Reno, Nevada. Scott has had vast experience in the restaurant and food service industry. One of the key elements he believes in is giving people a unique and special experience so that it is memorable and they will want to return. He oversaw event food planning at the MGM Resort in Reno, Nevada, for a number of years, as well as opening and operating a number of successful restaurants.

Something Better—G. W. and Tina Chew. Chef Chew, as he is known, pastors the Fayetteville, Arkansas, Seventh-day Adventist Church and is the chef/director of a newly formed restaurant.

The Appleseed, Metro Ministries—About 30 years ago a group of men and women came together and realized that the cities must be reached. It included current General Conference president Ted Wilson and his wife, as well as the director of the restaurant, Luis Cadiz.

We have categorized our findings so that you can easily find the answers you are looking for. Furthermore, we tried to ask similar questions to each person so that we could give you perspective as you search for principles and keys to success.

Size: The average space of those institutions we contacted was approximately 2,200 square feet.

Average Meal Cost: $8-$10 per person

Location: In order to have high traffic for lunch, you need to be in or near a location where people work. Most have a daily delivery of fresh produce that they then prepare on-site.

d'Sozo—three miles from downtown. It was not in the restaurant district but rather in a fast-food area and was the only vegan restaurant in Wichita. The founders placed it there because a developer gave them an amazing deal that they couldn't refuse.

Nature's Bounty—Lake County, California, one of the poorest counties in California. Its managers had parents that lived in Angwin, so they opened one nearby so that they could see their parents. Sharon Christensen was food service director at Weimar and started the vegan culinary program there.

Scott Beckett—He believes that with a restaurant, location is the most important element.

The Appleseed—The location of a restaurant should be in the city where there are a great number of people passing by it. The idea is to have people "fall into the restaurant." Wellness centers should be in the country, in "rural districts." The staff are better off if they live in the country, not too far from the city (see *Testimonies for the Church,* vol. 7, pp. 55, 60).

Average Number of Customers Served Daily

For the typical fast-food establishment we interviewed, the average lunch serves 500 or more people per day.

d'Sozo—70-90 per day

Nature's Bounty—35 per day

The Appleseed—100-150 per day

Employees

Volunteer workers program—d'Sozo, an Adventist-run restaurant in Wichita, Kansas, discovered that legally it couldn't operate a restaurant with volunteers. The IRS imposed a large per-day fine if they continued with volunteer staff.

Scott Beckett—"Cooks are hard to find. It is a stressful job, and they don't get paid very much. But if you can find people who believe in the mission, you will have a good chance of finding excellent talent for less than what it would typically cost.

"One of the biggest issues is people not showing up for work. At times you have to work with whom you've got, because it is a consistent issue of finding dependable employees. Once again, the mission-minded individual will be more dedicated."

When asked if they could give anyone looking to start a restaurant as a ministry some advice, they said it would be:

"Create a clear vision for what you want from your restaurant. Think out every single detail before you even identify a location. Do more research than you have ever done before. You must do your homework.

"The majority of restaurants are underfunded. The key is to have the proper funding and the ability to find talented staff."

Greatest Obstacles

d'Sozo—generating enough business to cover ongoing costs
Nature's Bounty—continually meeting food safety standards

Type of Clientele

d'Sozo—a lot of businesspeople with a passing interest in health but not necessarily vegetarians. Some travelers have found them on Web sites, such as Happy Cow or VegGuide. Seventy percent of the customers are female—nonworking or retired.

The Appleseed—New York City has many vegetarians. Others are professionals, working near the Wall Street area. A breakfast and lunch operation is preferable to a night operation, since most customers do not live near their workplace.

Marketing Efforts

d'Sozo—You have to advertise to keep the restaurant in people's minds. D'Sozo printed up flyers—half-page single side with a simple shot of Wichita's only French-trained chef—then stood outside office buildings and passed them out. The flyer mentioned that the restaurant was vegan but did not stress it. The restaurant received good press from dining magazines, airlines, a local television station that featured the chef, and newspaper articles. The management wished that they'd advertised on the university campus and felt that they should have gotten more involved in the vegan community/society.

Nature's Bounty—They relied primarily on word of mouth but did advertise in the newspaper/radio/TV. They also offered a cooking demo but had limited success, although only charging $10-$15 per ticket.

The Appleseed—During the remodeling phase the restaurant placed a "coming soon" sign in the window, then installed a permanent sign at the entrance. Word of mouth was very effective, though management felt that Adventist radio promotion would be helpful. Since a lot more people today are looking for healthful food, phone-book ads may work well in some cities. Good-tasting food and friendly staff are probably all that's necessary for advertisement.

Here is a news story surrounding the launch of The Appleseed in New York City:

Appleseed Restaurant Featured on Channel 4 Program

"Ted Wilson, director of Metro Ministries, appeared in a segment of WNBC-TV's *First Estate* program on Sunday, January 11 [1981]. Interviewer Dr. Russell Barber's questions centered on Appleseed Restaurant, the first denominationally sponsored vegetarian restaurant in New York City for many years. Opportunity was also given for Elder Wilson to explain Adventist beliefs and, in particular, the significance of the name Seventh-day Adventist.

"In the week following the segment's airing, a number of viewers called the restaurant, and twenty new people visited the Wall Street area establishment for lunch as a direct result of watching the program.

"Two calls were also received from viewers specifically interested in a statement Pastor Wilson made during the program indicating Adventist interest in opening additional restaurants in the metropolitan area. Both of these callers owned restaurants (one located in

Atlantic City, New Jersey) and expressed interest in having Seventh-day Adventists take them over" (in *Atlantic Union Gleaner,* Feb. 10, 1981, p. 7).

Type of Food/Cuisine/Menu and Type of Service Method

The biggest lesson we gleaned from all whom we interviewed was to be consistent with recipes so that when a person came in every Thursday, for example, they could order the same thing and know that it would taste the same way it did the week before. The latest trends and success stories involve restaurants such as Chipotle and Subway, in which customers can quickly walk through line, choose their ingredients, and quickly get their food.

d'Sozo—all vegan, some organic. Five-star international cuisine. Customers formed a line in front of the counter where they would order and pay. Staff then delivered the food to their table.

Nature's Bounty—all organic and not so much local, as it wasn't as important back then.

Scott Beckett—He believes the layout and functionality of the kitchen are key to success. In the restaurants he has set up and started he would create the menu before designing and laying out the kitchen. It ensured a smooth operation in which all employees can work seamlessly and not get into each other's way. The menu should even determine your location. It is important to keep the menu standardized so that you don't have too much daily turnover in ingredients. This keeps the preparation of food efficient.

We asked Scott how often a menu should be updated or changed.

"It is key to keep track of what items are selling. Ask the customers what they like. When you develop new items, give them to customers free of charge for a few days to get feedback. Empower the consumer by seeking their involvement."

"As the customers love the food and the environment, people will come back again and again. They will then begin to ask why we do what we do."

The Appleseed—A simple menu: sandwiches, salad bar, soups, similar to fast-food restaurants. People in the workplace don't have much time to eat during their lunch hour. The idea is to get to know the repeat customers.

Food Supplier/Source Method

d'Sozo—Sysco

Nature's Bounty—Veritable Vegetable and UNFI

Extra Services Offered

d'Sozo—The health food store was stocked with items from "The Tree of Life." It never realized a significant profit, as it needed more oversight than we gave it. There was a separate room in the health food store called a counseling room with a desk and a couch. The idea was to have physicians and therapists come who would give free medical counseling on Thursdays. Also, it had been set up for hydrotherapy and massage treatments. Management thought it could have been successful, though not as a high-volume/leading feature. Instead, it would have appealed to customers who had come to know the restaurant.

Nature's Bounty—It did a few catered events, but this can get so busy that it can distract from the mission.

Education Classes and Outreach

d'Sozo—They had cooking classes in the evenings. The baking classes didn't draw as many people. They tried combining children's cooking and health classes. Although it was not hands on, everyone would taste the food and then the physician would give a 45-minute presentation on a health topic. The management charged about $15 for them. Also, they ran cooking classes for three consecutive weeks for $150. The dishes prepared weren't arranged as a single meal. Instead, students made their own and then took it home.

- Cooking classes ran every month.
- Health lectures ran every other week.
- Kids' cooking classes were given twice per week.
- Little contests at classes gave everyone a chance to win at least once. The prizes consisted of magabooks, etc.

Simple kindness opened doors the best. The staff did nice things for people's birthdays as well. They found that the best secret was to be generous. They also had a rack of magabooks for sale. Every table had tracts that they had printed up, incorporating NEWSTART and an explanation of how everything works together. Also, each table had a little letter holder for more information.

Something Better—The restaurant offers seminars and cooking classes and meal plans that make it easy for people to adopt an entirely new lifestyle in a simple way with prepared meals.

The Appleseed—health books and leaflets, special sessions related to health such as a five-day smoking-cessation plan in the evening, personal testimony.

Number and Type of Employees

d'Sozo—12/Bible instructors primarily

Nature's Bounty—"We could feed up to 50 with two people working 9:00 a.m.-3:00 p.m. For breakfast we served smoothies. The division of labor in our restaurant was this: head person—cook and manager; second person—cashier, juice maker, serving of meals, vegetable preparation, and dishwashing during slow times. We did use disposable table service. Employees were younger home-schooled Adventists and Jehovah's Witnesses."

The Appleseed—five experienced older personnel doing cooking, younger persons serving. "It's better to have only Adventist help."

Mentoring/Education With Staff/Employees

d'Sozo—"We did have a prayer first thing in the morning, and some longer 'prayer meeting'-type occasions; but to be honest, it never reached its full potential, because of too many varying schedules. This is one reason I believe as strongly as I do in the country outpost concept. Unfortunately, we never had one, so people lived here and there with no common base for really establishing the kind of group spiritual life that I believe would be beneficial.

That's one thing that I would want to do different. I'm almost of the opinion that the outpost should be acquired first, but I think that the Lord could still work things out as He might wish. Still, a shared spiritual life and experience is vital, and we never achieved what I would have liked in that regard."

Nature's Bounty—"We mentored as staff worked with the head chef. Prayed with some of employees on a semiregular basis. Played instrumental religious music in the restaurant."

Most Important Lessons Learned

d'Sozo—They initially tried running the restaurant until 7:00 p.m. each day, but it wasn't a good idea. Management thought they should have focused more on the health food store.

Nature's Bounty—We began it based on personal love for cooking but realized an education on how to run a commercial kitchen and how to cook is a must. "We started small enough and realized capital is key. Without enough capital you are always trying to catch up. We broke even, but it was not easy in such a small town. We also provide spiritual food in a palatable way."

Scott Beckett—When he first went to a plant-based diet, his wife and he assumed that they would have to give up their taste buds. This has been the biggest obstacle in healthy vegetarian cooking. It has to taste good.

The Appleseed—A cafeteria-style operation is easier to run. The idea is to make friends with people. A combination of health food store, small food service (cafeteria style), and fresh produce has been very successful in San Juan, Puerto Rico, though management is not Adventist. Mayagüez, Puerto Rico, has two well-patronized cafeteria-style restaurants operated by Adventists.

It's not easy to get experienced personnel to operate the restaurant. Rents in the cities can be expensive.

Hours of Operation

d'Sozo—11:00 a.m.-3:00 p.m. for lunch. The health food store was open 9:00 a.m.-6:00 p.m. Sunday through Friday.

Advice:

d'Sozo—Structure the restaurant under an educational model, not a business one. Run it as a culinary school, but that has to be separate and distinct from the restaurant, and service times would have to be limited. This would be a nonprofit.

Nature's Bounty—Get more education. Take an online chef course: 18 lessons, 10-15 hours per lesson, $3,000 broken down into monthly payments. "If I had it to do over, I'd make sure to have a short, thought-provoking quote—biblical, Ellen White, or from medical or nutritional authorities—on each table and change it daily or weekly. They would be conversation starters or the thought for the day for those eating alone. In a metropolitan area one could sell several health/vegan food-related magazines. I think I'd save the books for personal contacts to be given away as opportunities presented themselves. This is what we did. It seems that giving too many books too early overwhelm and send a negative message to a secular public. Many people are reading less and relying on pictures or the abbreviated text on an iPad instead. Other points:

"Prime focus would be vegan eatery, breakfast/lunch, no dinner.

"People like choices but not too many—they want food fast and then relax.

"Need someone on team who could mix with clients.

"Weak point was customer interaction.

"Build friendships and then be extremely professional with cooking classes.

"Need station chefs for soups/sandwiches/bakery.

"Most important is that the food tastes good. People like comfort foods and are in a hurry. They want quality for their dollar.

"Have reading material available. Position a free-magazine rack by the door. If I was to do it over again, I would have something for sale such as *Vibrant Life* and perhaps also a non-Adventist thing. Could also have some quotes on the table in Plexiglas to get people thinking.

"Plan to cater to gluten-free—they will bring the rest of their group.

"Go to a Natural Products expo. They average 50,000 attendees."

Scott Beckett—"Make your customer happy. There is an old maxim: 'If people like something, they tell three people. If they don't like it, they tell 10.'

"With the economy as it is now, many restaurants are closing and thus offer opportunities to set up another for far less than it would actually cost to start from scratch.

"Most restaurants fail because they are undercapitalized. They do not have enough money to begin the restaurant. Every restaurant needs six months of working capital before you even open the doors.

"Margins in a restaurant are very narrow, and this is why 70-80 percent of them fail. Industry averages say that 35 percent of your expenses go to food costs and another 35 percent to labor. A restaurant or food service entity can be destroyed just based on lack of portion control. Consistent portions are key to budgeting and success. Another thing to consider and pay attention to is waste. If stuff is being thrown away, that could be your profits.

"When pricing and planning your menu, it is crucial that you get down-to-the-minute details, as specific as how many pieces of lettuce you will put in a dish. Each plate should be priced out to the penny. If the plate costs you $3 in food, then you have to charge at least $9 to break even in light of the 35 percent principle.

"Typically food costs get made up in sodas, alcohol, etc. Obviously that is not possible in an Adventist-run restaurant.

"So in light of this, what are ways to increase profit margin? Carbohydrate-based dishes are cheaper to create. Pasta is a great example of a place to make more profit. Once you get into such details as homemade mayonnaise, ketchup, cheeses, etc., this is where the costs can get out of control."

Something Better—G. W. Chew believes that his restaurant is a ministry, and the lives being changed testify to this fact. His favorite quote is "The conversion of souls is the one aim and object of restaurant work" (*Manuscript Releases,* vol. 8, p. 171).

He has concluded that becoming a blessing and friend to the community is key if you want to really make a difference. He shared that being open six days and closing on Sabbath really does make a statement.

The high point of the ministry so far has been their "lifestyle challenge" to the community. In conjunction with Sanare Life and Nyse Collins, who currently has a show on 3ABN, they decided to ask people to get a health checkup/blood test before and after the challenge in order to see the difference that their diet makes.

As all of this was taking place, literature evangelists visited the community with health books for sale and invitations to the challenge being held at the restaurant. Needless to say, people lost weight and saw dramatic improvements in their health.

What was so amazing about the restaurant was that a pastor was running it and working in conjunction with literature evangelists who were inviting the community to a sustained ministry that operated year-round.

We asked Pastor Chew if any Bible studies have begun. He shared that as a result of building a strong relationship with the community the prophecy-related Bible studies were very well attended, and numbers actually increased each night of the meetings.

Country Life Case Study

Many have heard of a venture that still has entities operating under the name of Country Life. Country Life was one of the most ambitious efforts we have ever seen to reach the cities with the gospel. Having learned a little more about its experience, we can say that clearly those involved had a sense of urgency that Jesus is coming and had devoted their entire lives to the finishing of God's work. They chose restaurants, health food manufacturing, lifestyle centers, and more to fulfill the calling of reaching the cities.

As we spoke with those involved with Country Life, we were amazed to hear how God led them in their efforts. They told of restaurant locations opening up in London, New York City, Paris, Tokyo, and the list could go on. The Lord was providentially working to get centers of influence into the cities around the world. As these restaurants would open up, beautiful estates would be offered for free or at far below cost that they could use as lifestyle centers. We heard stories of castles in Europe and Napoleon's vacation estate and more.

Also we learned a few important things as to why the venture of Country Life did not later continue to grow and expand as it had in its infancy. As we know, the devil always seems to be in the details. In the lessons we learned we found principles that we need to consider as we all look to reach the cities.

Here are the two most important ones we discovered from speaking with those who spearheaded Country Life.

1. **People are key.** If we build ministries or churches or restaurants dependent on one person or a small group of talents, what happens if someone gets sick or dies or leaves the faith? Suppose someone acts irresponsibly? If we have systems in place in which

the mission is so entwined into the fabric of the organization that no one person can deter it, then you will find success.

Make it a point to build a system so sound that if the manager is gone for a day or the main speaker decides to move on to something else, the ministry will continue without a problem. We can see that Country Life was too dependent on a few individuals to run such a large organization. Some of them left or moved on, and the organization lost its zeal and structure.

2. **Policies are vital.** They are the things that we all are not too excited about at the beginning of a new venture or ministry. After all, we all get along and love the Lord and don't see any issues that may arise down the road. The reality is that the devil is still seeking to cause havoc and block the mission of the remnant church.

In order to keep our mission constant and our ministries and ventures going forward, we must have sound policies in place.

What we saw with Country Life was that it did not have enough established policies so that one person's decisions or one person's opinion would not affect it.

The example we encountered several times was that a donated property was at times managed locally. When times got tough and there wasn't really a management or administrative staff, that manager would take on debt or sell a property to go a different route. It was a recipe for disaster.

Think about it. Someone has given us a castle as a resort for Seventh-day Adventists to bring sick people out of Paris to help them recover their health, show them how a farm works, and teach them how lifestyle changes can affect their health. Then times get tough, and you and I have 10 people on staff that we must pay, or perhaps we see some repairs that need to take place. The worst thing to do is to think that we can assume a little debt and then pay it back later. Time and time again such decisions took institutions out of the hands of Country Life's mission and one by one eliminated the treasures that God had given to the venture.

The good news is that we can learn from such mistakes and have better contracts and policies in place as we encounter opportunities such as those described above. If a large organization such as Country Life were to be attempted today, there would need to be a management structure that could help train and encourage staff around the world while at the same time serving as a property manager and lease holder so that no one person could affect in a negative way any property being used in the Lord's work.

SECTION 7:
Ministry of Lifestyle Reform/Outpost Health Resorts: Integrated Evangelism

The outpost is an amazing concept within the Beehive structure. Probably one of the most compelling examples is the country retreat occupied by Enoch. Scripture tells us that Enoch was translated. But the book of Jude says that Enoch was preaching a message regarding, not the first advent of Christ, but the second. In other words, Enoch was preaching the three angels' messages. According to Jude 14 and 15, Enoch prophesied and preached to the ungodly. From Ellen White we learn that Enoch did so from his retirement place (country dwelling or outpost), going into the city and bringing people out to nature where they could see the hand of God (see *Christ Triumphant,* p. 49). Some were converted and died in Christ before the Flood.

But the concept of an outpost did not end with Enoch. Before we had hospitals we called our medical institutions sanitariums. Ellen White counseled the church to build such health facilities outside of the cities, where people could come to receive simple, natural treatments. They would recover more effectively being in country settings, with land and beauty surrounding them.

The Lord has an objective behind the concept of an outpost. Notice the following statement:

"Great light has been shining upon us, but how little of this light we reflect to the world! Heavenly angels are waiting for human beings to cooperate with them in the practical carrying out of the principles of truth. It is through the agency of our sanitariums and kindred enterprises that much of this work is to be done. These institutions are to be God's memorials, where His healing power can reach all classes, high and low, rich and poor. Every dollar invested in them for Christ's sake will bring blessings both to the giver and to suffering humanity" (*Testimonies for the Church,* vol. 7, pp. 58, 59).

Did you catch that the prophet states that "heavenly angels are waiting for human beings to cooperate with them"? Cooperate with them how and in what? The answer is "in the practical carrying of the principles of truth." The words that follow are powerful: "It is through the agency of our sanitariums and kindred enterprises that much of this work is to be done."

Do you realize that Ellen White is saying that angels perform a task just like that involved in an outpost? It makes sense. God's angels work our planet of evil cities from an outpost— heaven. Their mission is to come to our cities with divine messages, but their home is out in the faraway country called heaven.

In the Beehive structure Ellen White counsels us to have outposts from which church members could go into the cities and share the warning message of the third angel. And after ministering to the sick in the cities, we can then invite them back to the outpost, where they can receive loving care from the medical missionary doctors and nurses, as well as other medical missionaries. Two more statements that make the divine objective even clearer:

"Our sanitariums are to be established for one object, the advancement of present truth. And they are to be so conducted that a decided impression in favor of the truth will be made on the minds of those who come to them for treatment. . . . We have a warning message to bear to the world, and our earnestness, our devotion to God's service, is to impress those who come to our sanitariums" (*ibid.,* p. 97).

"If a sanitarium connected with this closing message fails to lift up Christ and the principles of the gospel as developed in the third angel's message, it fails in its most important feature, and contradicts the very object of its existence" (in *Review and Herald,* Oct. 29, 1914).

Following are some additional characteristics necessary for a successful outpost.

Rural Location. "Those who plan to establish sanitariums should reason from cause to effect. They should lay their plans with a deep insight into the necessities of a medical institution. One of the first necessities is a site out of the city, in a retired place, where the institution can be surrounded by grounds that can be beautified with flowers and shrubs and trees" (in *Review and Herald,* Aug. 11, 1904).

"The Lord has been giving me light in regard to many things. He has shown me that our sanitariums should be erected on as high an elevation as is necessary to secure the best results, and that they are to be surrounded by extensive tracts of land, beautified by flowers and ornamental trees" (*Selected Messages,* book 2, p. 301).

We should follow the same principle. Back then they were about 90 minutes to two hours (15-20 miles) away from the large cities.

Size of Outpost. "Instead of investing in one medical institution all the means obtainable, we ought to establish smaller sanitariums in many places" (*Testimonies for the Church,* vol. 7, p. 98).

"Never, never build mammoth institutions. Let these institutions be small, and let there be more of them, that the work of winning souls to Christ may be accomplished" (*Medical Ministry,* p. 323).

Facilities Should Be Simple and Beautiful. We should be able to accommodate around 20 or so and the facilities should not be extravagant or carry any debt. If the unit has an excess of resources or is unusually successful, then establish other locations. The grounds should be well kept and attractive with ornamental plants near the buildings and trees a little way out from them. Plenty of sunshine and fresh air should permeate the buildings and bedrooms. The buildings should be homelike, not mammoth structures that are not easily duplicated. They should have lecture halls and a large area for cooking classes/health demonstrations.

"The Garden of Eden, the home of our first parents, was exceedingly beautiful. Graceful shrubs and delicate flowers greeted the eye at every turn. In the garden were trees of every variety, many of them laden with fragrant and delicious fruit. On their branches the birds caroled their songs of praise. Adam and Eve, in their untainted purity, delighted in the sights and sounds of Eden. And today, although sin has cast its shadow over the earth, God desires His children to find delight in the works of His hands. To locate our sanitariums amidst the scenes of nature would be to follow God's plan; and the more closely this plan is followed, the more wonderfully will He work to restore suffering humanity. For our educational and medical institutions, places should be chosen where, away from the dark clouds of sin that hang over the great cities, the Sun of Righteousness can arise, "with healing in his wings. Malachi 4:2" (*Testimonies for the Church,* vol. 7, p. 81).

Classes Should Be Varied. Not only should such institutions be places where healing can take place for the sick—they should also be training centers in which students, made up of both young and old, can learn alongside the sick while assisting in taking care of them. Classes should include agriculture, Bible study, health seminars, and cooking. And specifically for the students, there should be instruction in public speaking and evangelism, and trades such as carpentry and web and graphic design. The various options will help medical missionary students become industrious and self-supporting.

Costs. The costs for the students should be as affordable as possible. Those for the patients should be standard and fair but allow for some who may not be able to pay the full fees. God will make up the difference—He always does.

Products/Affiliations. The outposts can sell their agricultural products to the city mission vegetarian restaurants. At the same time, the treatment rooms (health spas) affiliated with the city mission will act as sources of new clients along with the other ministries in the city.

Staff/Salaries. The staff of the health retreats should receive fair wages according to national standards, and when they have a surplus, all should share it as a blessing and an incentive to continue their hard work.

Caring for the ill is difficult labor, with early hours and late nights. Sick guests do not follow normal sleep patterns. As a result, staff can burn out quickly. Management should enter such programs intelligently and prayerfully with the supreme goal being good health and temperance for all, including employees. Rotate duties to allow the staff members themselves to actually live the healthful lifestyle promoted throughout the outpost health retreat.

Care of Health Guests. Be prompt to appointments and be open and honest with each client. Men should work with men and women with women. Be fully transparent in all actions.

Health Resorts, Farms, and Education. We could say so much about education that it could fill up many books. In fact, if you have not done so, read the book *Education,* by Ellen White. It is full of practical reasons as to why God has always endorsed an educational system based on biblical principles and why it is so important today.

But those involved with Christian education have expressed a growing concern that the costs are slowly becoming so expensive that many families just cannot afford it. As we look at the world today, perhaps the time has come to consider more broadly the many types of educational institutions that we can offer. Rather than reach a point in the future when the majority of Seventh-day Adventists cannot afford Christian education, perhaps now is the time to look at some alternatives. Below we have included some quotes on more simple and affordable methods of education that may find a broader application around the globe than what we have been considering until now.

"Agriculture is the ABC of industrial education" (*Manuscript Releases,* vol. 2, p.74).

"We are to establish schools away from the cities, where the youth can learn to cultivate the soil, and thus help to make themselves and the school self-supporting. Let means be gathered for the establishment of such schools. In connection with these schools, work is to be done in mechanical and agricultural lines. All the different lines of work that the situation of the place will warrant are to be brought in" (*ibid.,* pp. 64, 65).

"Wise plans are to be laid for the cultivation of the land. The students are to be given a practical education in agriculture. This education will be of inestimable value to them in their future work. Thorough work is to be done in cultivating the land, and from this the students are to learn how necessary it is to do thorough work in cultivating the garden of the heart" (in *Review and Herald,* Sept. 1, 1904).

"There is need of intelligence and educated ability to devise the best methods in farming, in building, and in every other department, that the worker may not labor in vain" (*That I May Know Him,* p. 333).

Though perhaps some of the trades of yesteryear, such as blacksmithing or carpentry, may no longer be common today, there is never going to come a time that food will become obsolete. More and more as we see the control of food slipping into the hands of corporate agribusiness, we should consider the need to get our schools onto programs that grow food locally.

Seventh-day Adventists profess that the day will come when religious liberty will become extinct and that in that time we will have to accept the mark of the beast or reject it. If our desire is to reject it, then we need to begin finding ways to make our institutions and schools and families independent of the food supply system. This would offer our schools true freedom and independence.

As we seek to reach the cities, it will create a growing need for restaurants, health food manufacturers, health food stores, and more. If that is the case, then the schools and individuals who have been educated to raise food will be able to sell it to those desiring the finest food products and produce. Consider the ways that a local farm run by a Seventh-day Adventist high school or college could provide employment for students and integrate an agricultural component into the educational process.

Other ideas to consider for both our institutions and for individuals are such programs as Community Supported Agriculture. The growing trend involves someone with farmland contracting with local residents to provide fresh produce every week or month during the harvest season. The customers thus become active supporters of the farm.

The Industry of Publishing. As we witness culture changing from print to digital, many wonder if the printing press is an obsolete technology. But if we consider the fact that if a government wanted to, it could shut off the Internet. And that is exactly what has taken place in the past few years with the events taking place in the Middle East and elsewhere. The printed page still has a life of its own. It does not need batteries to work and thus can last for a lifetime.

"Our publishing work was established by the direction of God and under His special supervision. It was designed to accomplish a specific purpose. Seventh-day Adventists have been chosen by God as a peculiar people, separate from the world. By the great cleaver of truth He has cut them out from the quarry of the world and brought them into connection with Himself. He has made them His representatives and has called them to be ambassadors for Him in the last work of salvation. The greatest wealth of truth ever entrusted to mortals, the most solemn and fearful warnings ever sent by God to man, have been committed to them to be given to the world; and in the accomplishment of this work our publishing houses are among the most effective agencies" (*Testimonies for the Church*, vol. 7, p. 138).

"These institutions [publishing houses] are to stand as witnesses for God, teachers of righteousness to the people. From them truth is to go forth as a lamp that burneth. Like a great light in a lighthouse on a dangerous coast, they are constantly to send forth beams of light into the darkness of the world, to warn men of the dangers that threaten them with destruction" (*ibid.*).

The materials we produce today and in the future should be noticeably unique—not just to be that way but in the sense that people should know they are reading a Seventh-day Adventist pamphlet by its bold adherence to the Word of God.

"The publications sent forth from our printing houses are to prepare a people to meet God. Throughout the world they are to do the same work that was done by John the Baptist for the Jewish nation. By startling messages of warning, God's prophet awakened men from worldly dreaming. Through him God called backsliding Israel to repentance. By his presentation of truth he exposed popular delusions. In contrast with the false theories of his time, truth in his teaching stood forth as an eternal certainty. 'Repent ye: for the kingdom of heaven is at hand' was John's message. Matthew 3:2. This same message, through the publications from our printing houses, is to be given to the world today" (*ibid.*, p. 139).

"And in a large degree through our publishing houses is to be accomplished the work of that other angel who comes down from heaven with great power and who lightens the earth with his glory" (*ibid.*, p. 140).

The Mission in Practice . . . Words From the Front Line
James Rafferty, cofounder, Lightbearers Ministry

What led you to the publishing work rather than another area of ministry?
"I began in the preaching ministry which led to publishing what we were learning."

Why is print still a valid form of evangelism in a world of technology?
"Mainly because so many millions of people still do not have access to technology."

What advice can you give to someone who feels called to the publishing work?
"Start where you are with what you have. We began in a home with a copy machine."

SECTION 8:
Ministry of Integrated Personal Evangelism

"Evangelism" has become a word that many avoid, both verbally and functionally. It seems to conjure up many ill feelings—fear, doubt, indifference, and skepticism—in some minds. Some even say that it doesn't work anymore. One could imagine that during the time of Christ, if He only spoke a sermon from the mount all the time, He too would have had His challenges. But it seems that we have relegated evangelism—the seeking of lost human beings for Christ—to a one-approach, one-shot drudgery. In Matthew 23:23 and Luke 11:42 Christ presents a principle that we must not forget. He points out that while the Pharisees should have tithed, "these are the things you should have done without neglecting the others" (NASB). In other words, yes, we should have large evangelistic series, but we ought not neglect personal, relational evangelism. The Beehive's multifaceted ministry facilitates the personal Christlike touch of relational evangelism.

Clearly Christ spent the majority of His time with the people in their homes, shops, and other places of employment, social or festive gatherings, etc. He was right where they were, seeking them out and talking to them about "higher things." Today most workplaces and areas of social gathering prohibit proselytizing. And although freedom of expression is still legal, Christians are limited in how openly they can share their faith in Christ. The challenge then is to find ways around this obstacle.

Integrated Ministry. God is moving to expand and integrate Adventist-Laymen's Services and Industries (ASI) as a facet of the Beehive concept. Through enterprising ventures we create the marketplace, destinations, and meeting spots where people can experience the love of Jesus seen in His people, often while dining together on delicious, healthful meals. This, too, is evangelism. It is ministry integration on the corporate level, such as what took place in the Bay Area Beehive.

As we began the Beehive our first enterprise was a thrift store. But it could be other marketplace ventures, according to the model demonstrated in the Bay Area back in 1901. It could be a café, vegetarian restaurant, a health food store, or a smoothie shop. We chose a thrift store because it is a good business model, gets the church members involved through clothing drives and volunteering, and attracts a cross section of people. And a thrift store boldly demonstrates what the mission is while earning the respect of the people. So when it states that the proceeds go to help fight the obesity epidemic in our country (or whatever your mission is), people feel as if they are helping. By the way, this makes it easy to invite them to health seminars and cooking classes. The key is to always incorporate health in the discourse, using it as the right arm of the gospel.

Integrated personal evangelism is at the heart of what we describe as "The Brand-new Old Idea"—a method used by the Son of God Himself! And when you employ the Christocentric method of mingling with the people, caring for their needs, engaging them in wholesome conversation about higher things, you can then invite them to the "sermon on the mount." You tell them what your personal experience has been like following Him. Then the atmosphere is more conducive to inviting them to follow your example. And because they have seen your love and experienced your care, they are more likely to accept an invitation to traditional evangelistic meetings. Their hearts have been softened. Matthew 4:23-25 portrays Christ's approach to people:

"And Jesus went about all Galilee, teaching in their synagogues, and preaching the gospel of the kingdom, and healing all manner of sickness and all manner of disease among the people. And his fame went throughout all Syria: and they brought unto him all sick people that were taken with divers diseases and torments, and those which were possessed with devils, and those which were lunatick, and those that had the palsy; and he healed them."

What happens next is amazing.

"And there followed him *great multitudes* of people from Galilee, and from Decapolis, and from Jerusalem, and from Judaea, and from beyond Jordan."

Study the Needs of the City. It is necessary to study each locale to see what specific needs it has. In Atlanta our first integrated project took place in a 14,000-square-foot retail space of a shopping mall. When the Beehive expanded to Arizona, it employed a college campus lecture hall at Arizona State University. Then the Arizona Beehive began to conduct meetings and training out of a local conference church. A developing hive in Orlando started with college students meeting on a nearby hospital campus. Hospital employees and the families of patients often attend. Each city and its Beehive will have individual requirements. Cities in the South of the U.S. that are more familiar with Christianity may be approached differently than those of the West or the Northeast.

Starting at a neutral location is ideal. It is the perfect environment to accomplish a threefold objective: revival and reformation, training, and evangelism. Your storefront or place of business can be multipurpose and double as a meeting place. In Atlanta we used the thrift store location as the space for medical missionary training. To finish His work, God's people must be trained and equipped. But before that can happen, they must experience revival to the extent that they see their own spiritual needs as well as their responsibility to seek the lost, something that must happen in every Beehive within the city. So the objective should always include helping God's people experience repentance, revival, and reformation. It is the greatest requirement of the church today.

We rarely want to go out and mingle with the people. For a variety of reasons, most church members don't really want to do much in the way of outreach. Some struggle with issues of health, diet, and self-control, and they need repentance and revival in their lives. It is no secret that we become complacent and too comfortable and make our local churches a place to have weekly events for spiritual entertainment. The harvest is ripe, but there is a famine in the land for the Word of God. How ironic! We must hear God's Word to be able to share it. It is impossible to give others what we don't possess or even understand. But we must also have reformation, because if a person is dead and you revive them, only for them to go back to what they were doing before, they will die again. So we need to have all three facets, and it has worked well for the Beehive when we invite church members from the surrounding local churches to come out on Friday evenings to the revival seminars and get out of their comfort zones.

Once we had established Friday and Saturday night meetings focusing on revival and reformation, church members began to bring friends, colleagues, and neighbors who would never have been comfortable entering a church building.

The next step in the Beehive process, after people are experiencing revival and reformation and doing their own personal evangelism by bringing friends to the meetings, is to start training individuals to go to work. That's the ministry of house-to-house labor—the role of the literature evangelist, Bible instructor, and medical missionary.

The Mission in Practice . . . Words From the Front Line

Chad Stuart, pastor of the Visalia Seventh-day Adventist Church in Visalia, California; pastor and leader of the ARK, a thriving church plant.

We spoke with a number of pastors and asked them what their secrets were for growing their church and using unique cutting-edge methods to lead others to Christ. Of all those we spoke with, none were as exciting and successful as that of the one following.

What are the most effective methods of integrated evangelism your church is using in the twenty-first century?

A young minister in the Central California Conference of Seventh-day Adventists reports that "God is definitely blessing out here. In about four years we've had more than 90 baptisms/ profession of faith. Our attendance has doubled, and we've added 160 members total (so our growth is more than 50 percent evangelistic). Also, we've started a church plant. So with all that in mind, here are my three most important elements of how a church can be effective with their evangelistic outreach:

1. **Prayer.** While it should be self-explanatory, unfortunately it is primarily lip service in the process of evangelism. But we bathe things in prayer. We have individuals that pray from 8:30 a.m. till 10:00 a.m. every Sabbath morning during the first service. A special prayer group also prays at the ARK (our church plant) from 4:30 p.m. to 5:30 p.m.

   "Also we have prayer meetings. Every single person attached to our church is on a list. That list is divided up among 67 prayer warriors in our church, and each person gets prayed for *daily!* We pray for specific things such as God's protection and help, but also that each person will be an evangelist for Jesus! I've seen a difference.

2. **"The second key is that we preach and teach the *entire* message of the Bible** (aka the *entire* Seventh-day Adventist message). We don't water down anything. God will not honor unfaithful teaching! At times we may have music that seems progressive and our order of service may be different; and we may format evangelism sometimes in unique ways, but people will hear about the Sabbath as God's only day and the sanctuary doctrine. They will become familiar with the name of Ellen White, will know that we pay tithe, and that we as the remnant have a great responsibility.

3. **"We train kindness**—i.e., we emphasize it all the time. Our greeters go through a greeters training program. Constantly we affirm our congregation when someone joins and talks about how nice this church is. Furthermore, we've built a welcome center. I do an 'in community time' to build warmth into the service, sort of an informal chat time with the congregation.

4. **"The fourth key is to have a good Bible instructor.** I am not talking about the one that is here for six months and then gone, but find a great one and hold on to him or her. We've done that, and what a blessing!

   "Most of our evangelism has been done out of the weekly Sabbath service. So far we've held only one full reaping campaign. The rest of our growth has been encouraging our members to bring friends and family to church, and then together we connect with them and get them into Bible studies."

David Asscherick, cofounder, ARISE

What are the three most cutting-edge twenty-first-century methods of public evangelism in your opinion?

"My answer is super-simple and short:

"**Truth** (Jesus and His Word).

"**Time** (Relationships take time and are essential, especially in the age in which we live today. We need to invest in people. This takes time, no two ways about it.)

"**Trust** (We've got to trust people and be trusted by them. It takes real investment and energy. Also, it demands time.)"

SECTION 9:
Ministry to the Prisons

While the name Beehive comes from the inspired dream given to Ellen G. White, its emotional center and core belief system derives from the fifty-eighth chapter of Isaiah. In it we see God summoning His people to a fast. But it is not one that abstains from food. Nor is it a formal religious ceremony. The first part of the fast that God is calling His people to in these final days is to "let the oppressed go free, and that ye break every yoke." A yoke is bondage. Jesus came to break every yoke of those who were in bondage. He set the captives free by preaching deliverance to them. So must those who seek to follow after the divine pattern set before them.

This is prison ministry. But the days of going to jails and singing a few songs and reading a text or two are over. We are in the final moments of our earth's history and need to do what God has called His people to do: to go into the prisons and, while free ourselves, become fellow bondmen and bondwomen with those incarcerated.

Of the "least of these" outlined in Matthew 25, integrated personal evangelism explicitly applies to two categories. For every other category it is possible to witness from afar, as many of us do. Yes, it is true, that many, instead of physically mingling with spiritually lost human beings, will send money or support someone else who is doing it. For example, for the person who is hungry, we can supply money or food and never have to see them. The same goes for those who are thirsty in some developing country and who need water wells. You can do the same for the person who is without clothes. You just send them. And as for the stranger, technically you can take them in by paying for a room at a motel. Probably more do that than actually invite them into their own homes. We can accomplish the divine commission just by using money or other resources. However, the last two, as mentioned in chapter 2, require that personal touch that Christ demonstrated. In Matthew 25:36 Jesus says: "I was sick, and ye visited me: I was in prison, and you came unto me."

Here Christ Himself distinguishes between the first four categories and the last two. As if progressively fulfilling His divine character, the call is to get progressively closer to the people wherever they are, including in prison. We should invite even the stranger in. But if you find a way around that, we still need to personally visit the sick and go into the prison to share the love of God with someone who may have no hope. While the other categories are not to be left undone, visiting the sick and ministering to those in prison is the final work that God asks the Beehive concept and ministry to fulfill. Notice what the Bible says:

"Remember them that are in bonds, *as bound with them*; and them which suffer adversity, as being yourselves also in the body" (Heb. 13:3).

Paul says that we are to be in bounds with them. Now ,does that mean we are to be locked up in prison with them? No, not at all. The Bible uses the word "as." As being so close to them that it is just as if you are yourself in prison. Ellen G. White had an opportunity to experience firsthand the blessing of visiting prisoners and sharing encouragement:

"During my stay in Oregon I visited the prison in Salem, in company with Brother and Sister Carter and Sister Jordan. When the time arrived for service, we were conducted to the chapel, which was made cheerful by an abundance of light and pure, fresh air. At a signal from the bell, two men opened the great iron gates, and the prisoners came flocking in. The doors were securely closed behind them, and for the first time in my life I was immured in prison walls.

"I had expected to see a set of repulsive-looking men, but was disappointed; many of them seemed to be intelligent, and some to be men of ability. They were dressed in the coarse but neat prison uniform, their hair smooth, and their boots brushed. As I looked upon the varied physiognomies before me, I thought: 'To each of these men have been committed peculiar gifts, or talents, to be used for the glory of God and the benefit of the world; but they have despised these gifts of heaven, abused, and misapplied them'" (*Testimonies for the Church*, vol. 4, p. 292).

One could imagine that the preconceived notions that even Ellen White had during her visit are what most would have when visiting a prison. Notice that she was expecting one thing and experienced something totally different. Even the prophet had to realize that even men who had "misapplied" gifts and talents were individuals to be saved.

This ministry is not a call to go to the prisons and feel some deep sympathy for those whose lives have gone astray. Rather, it is a summons to follow Christ completely and receive understanding of His divine strategy to reach the world. Most have never considered that Christ's two great final acts were to heal and to give hope to a prisoner. Each sought to make a lasting impression. And certainly for the thief on the cross, it has. You would be hard pressed to find someone who hasn't heard about him.

The thief on the cross, through his supplication, has spoken to millions far from Calvary. It is the belief of the Beehive that Jesus will use prisoners in the same way today. Their desperate requests from behind iron bars will reach millions that the church cannot otherwise begin to touch. It has happened again and again. When a prisoner reads our literature and begins to study as a result, they invariably want a loved one to hear the truth that they have learned. While they cannot send the material themselves, they often request someone from the outside either to mail material to a family member or friend or to visit them. God's people need to take full advantage of this opportunity in these closing moments.

The issue is that most of our individual prison ministries cannot take literature into the prisons for distribution. They can only go in and share something from the Bible and a song, but cannot leave anything for the prisoner. However, a publisher can send material into the prison at the request of the inmate or by the prison chaplain. The time has come to unite with groups that can get such material into the prisons or start entities that can gain approval for such literature distribution.

Gospel workers, i.e., literature evangelists, Bible instructors, and medical missionaries, need to be ready to enter the prisons and share the three angels' messages. We need to compile mailing lists from the prisoners' desperate requests. For every person trapped in a hellish prison cell there are five to 10 relatives or friends who are equally trapped in a life of sin. So prison ministries do not just focus on prisoners, but share with them so that they too can minister to the world. "Go out quickly into the streets and lanes of the city, and bring in hither the poor, and the maimed, and the halt, and the blind. . . . Lord, it is done as thou hast commanded, and yet there is room. And the lord said unto the servant, Go out into the highways and hedges, and compel them to come in, that my house may be filled" (Luke 14:21-23).

The Mission in Practice . . . Words From the Front Line
Richard Bland, president, United Prison Ministries International (UPMI)

The Best Way to Do Prison Ministry:
"Prison ministry is being willing to take a risk to entangle with the devil's best! Present the Bible only, because men and women in prison do not trust or have confidence in people that claim to be Christians. They realize there are thousands of different denominations using the same Bible, but coming up with different answers. More often than not, they believe these Christians are being dishonest. The majority of prisoners see Christians as phony. Many times they buy their drugs and alcohol from people who go by the name of Christian. When they party on Saturday night, they see the same folks on Sunday morning at church."

What is the best way a local church can get involved?
"In light of the fact that prisoners don't have confidence in churches, it is best that a faithful, committed believer with a firm faith in the Bible should endeavor to begin prison ministry work as a direct assignment from God, but not necessarily on behalf of the church.

Create a name for a small group that is not related to the church, i.e., Alaska Prison Ministry instead of ABC Christian Church on Main Street.

"Prisoners do not care what people think—they want to know for sure what is truth, and this can be found only with a biblical basis. Go by the Book—go by the Bible.

"A great way to lead off any discussion is to share with them that they should not trust you (Jer. 17:5). They should trust only the Bible. Build their confidence in the Word of God. They will learn to listen to God's Word.

"Offer peace to them, which comes only from God.

"I will say right up front that this type of ministry is not for everyone. You are entering a place where you will come in contact with some of the devil's best.

"There are two groups of people that know the city very well. The first group is criminals, and the second group is taxicab drivers. Cities are naturally a breeding ground for criminal activity.

"Prisoners make some of the best evangelists. Jesus said the prostitute and the thief would enter before many. This is because they are risk takers and are willing to do what they believe in.

"God is in search of risk takers. For example, a prostitute fears nothing. She realizes any man could take her life in an instant. She gets into a car with a stranger who is going to exchange money for sex. How much bolder can you get? This is an extremely risky situation. God is looking for risk takers like this whom He can convert to His purposes. Saul became Paul. He was in essence a bounty hunter. God recognizes that when He finds a bold risk taker He can turn them into bold soul winners.

"The woman at the well is another example. Apparently she had such a bad reputation that other women did not associate with her. She would come to the well in the heat of the day to avoid the crowd. But Jesus meets her at the well and contrasts this woman of ill repute with His own disciples. He sent His disciples into town to witness for Him, but they came back with groceries. But the woman at the well came back with souls.

"Mary Magdalene was another risk taker. Prostitutes have no shame. They are bold, and when they obtain the Word of God they will share it as they would their drugs or bodies. Jesus is looking for people who are on fire for Him. He is not interested in lukewarm individuals.

"When a prisoner is planning to rob a bank, they know that after they do so, every police officer in the city will be looking for them. They realize ahead of time that it is either kill or be killed. Thus they are risk takers. How many people do you know that would show up to church next week even at the risk of 20 years in prison? Prisoners are bold and are needed in God's work.

"We need people willing to make a sacrifice. When Jesus was on the cross, the only one willing to stand for Him was a thief, a criminal.

"Prison ministry is about showing love to God. He tells us that if we visit those in prison, we visit Him."

Should prison ministry partner with other facets of the work, or should it stand alone?

"Seventy-five percent of all of UPMI Bible Study lessons are going to prisoners' families!

"The first time we ever went to a prison was to a group of 200 men. They asked me what the Bible says about eating pork, speaking in tongues, etc. After the meeting, the prisoners thought they had me cornered. The Lord then impressed me to meet with a smaller group of just 10 men each week to make a real difference in their lives.

"Fifteen men showed up the next week. The Lord impressed us to teach them what we knew so that they would be the leaders on the inside if we were never to come back. As we expected, because we were teaching truth from the Bible, the authorities told us not to come back. But in six months, after studying with just those 15 men, we had 18,000 Bible studies going on. We gave these men a high calling and told them that they were the watchmen of Ezekiel 33. Many of them knew how to reach people via their old lives in gangs, etc.

"We told them that they had a duty to share with anyone they came in contact with or they were stealing from them. They had been given something for the purpose of sharing, and now they had to share it—otherwise they were stealing. That is how the gospel is. It was given to us to share with others. If we don't share it, we're stealing. This impressed upon them a sense of duty. They told their fellow prisoners, and then after six months, the word had spread to 27 states. All we did was show up and share the truth.

"As of today we have distributed more than 71 million tracts in prisons worldwide. When we empower prisoners with the Bible, they become evangelists. We teach prisoners never to trust human beings but only the Bible. They are no longer pushing dope—they are pushing the Advent hope.

"We are not allowed to send materials to prisoners or their families unless they first request studies. When that happens, we know that it is a result of the Holy Spirit."

Jared Thurmon, director, The Beehive International

"I had the opportunity during the past year to get involved with prison ministry. I can say that it's one of the most fulfilling I have been a part of. Let me share a few simple things if you are looking to set up a prison ministry in your church.

1. "**Study to see what the Bible says about visiting those in prison.** In summary, we are visiting Jesus. Have you ever considered that some of the greatest individuals in history have been prisoners at one time or another? Also remember that one day in the future many will be persecuted and imprisoned solely for believing in the Bible alone as the source of their faith. In other words, you or I may soon be a prisoner, so let's consider those already there.

2. "**Call the largest detention centers and/or prisons in your city and tell them you are a church seeking to minister to prisoners.** They will explain how to get started. It will include having a small group that can go to the prison and get a background check. Then you will have an orientation session about what things you can do, how to dress, what to say, and more.

3. "**Last but not least, make it count.** You are going to bring a breath of fresh air and hope to men and women closed up in a cell. What would you want someone to tell you if they came to visit you?

"In my own experience, knowing how long the prisoners will be there shapes what I tell them. At some detention centers they will remain just a few days to a couple weeks. If that is the case, you will most likely have only one opportunity to meet an individual person. Since you have only one hour with them and then in two weeks they will be out in the real world again, what is it you want to tell them? Or if they will be there for six months, giving you time to build a relationship, what topics should you study together?

"I have found that if I have only a short time with someone, I make sure to build the credibility of studying the Bible and tell them about such books as *The Great Controversy* that can help them understand Bible prophecy more in depth. In addition, I concentrate on topics vital to the relationship between one's physical and spiritual life.

"From what I have seen, such men and women love to sing and love to present their requests to God in prayer. Do not leave these aspects out of your prison ministry. For more information on effective prison ministry, look up United Prison Ministries International."

CHAPTER 8

CORPORATE EVANGELISM— FAITH AND WORK

t is fascinating to study the methods of Christ and His blueprint. Truly the Lord has left us an example that we should follow. He thought of everything down to the finest detail. Consider the calling of the Twelve. They were a diverse group of individuals: tax collector, fishermen, etc. And as the number of His disciples grew, it brought in more diversity, such as Luke the physician and Paul, a doctor of the law and a tentmaker. Their variety was essential to the success of the mission. Peter certainly had a different effect on people than, say, Paul. John could do what Stephen could not. But God had called them all together to be the disciples of the lowly Galilean preacher.

We could say that they in essence formed a company—a corporate body. For any business organization to function successfully, it must have a diversity of gifts. It has just as much need for janitors and mailroom clerks as CEOs. Together they fulfill the manifold roles and responsibilities of the single company mission. The mission of Christ is to lead human beings to God's kingdom through the gospel message. Paul speaks of the spectrum of gifts in 1 Corinthians 12 and Ephesians 4 that the members of the single body of Christ would receive. It is a blueprint idea especially for those seeking to do the final work in the cities.

Interestingly, there was another powerful effort in evangelism almost happening simultaneously during the late 1800s and early 1900s. While many of the activities of the Bay Area Beehive were gaining traction the concept of corporate evangelism was operating in the city of Chicago and having much success. Dr. John Harvey Kellogg had many working with him in what were known as "Christian Helpers Bands." In a General Conference sermon he shared his experiences with an audience of gospel ministers:

"A few months ago we organized, at the Sanitarium, a Christian Help Band, consisting of nine workers—a leader, a Bible worker, a missionary nurse, three missionary mothers, and three burden bearers. This plan gives opportunity for all kinds of talent. The leader looks up the work, presides at the weekly meetings, and makes reports. The Bible worker gives Bible readings where they will be appreciated. The missionary nurse does work where the sick are found. The missionary mothers see that household help and clothing are provided. The burden bearers (young men are well suited for this) split wood, do chores, etc." (John Harvey Kellogg, "Openings for Medical Missionary Work at Home and Abroad," General Morning Session, Feb. 14, 1893).

Notice that the nine workers included:

    (a) a leader

    (b) Bible instructor

    (c) missionary nurse

(d) three missionary mothers

(e) three burden bearers

What we see is not only a perfect picture of the church doing medical missionary projects, but corporate evangelism at its finest. Let's convert some of those categories to terms we're more familiar with and add a few that are relevant to our day:

(a) leader—pastor, local elder, deacon, medical missionary

(b) Bible instructor

(c) literature evangelist

(d) missionary nurse—nutritionist, dietitian, physical therapist, medical missionary, caregivers

(e) missionary mothers—nurturing women, homemakers, grandmothers

(f) missionary fathers—spiritual men, local elders/deacons, pastors

(g) burden bearers—plumbers, carpenters, electricians, roofers, mechanics, etc.

(h) missionary lawyers

(i) medical missionary physicians

Imagine the teams that we could put together today. With such a wealth of talent, skills, and professional experience in the church, and with the outpouring of the Holy Spirit, we could see the kind of results witnessed in the early church. Do you see the pattern given by Christ to utilize the diversity of talents to reach all types with their various needs?

The Christian Helpers Bands would divide the city of Chicago up into districts and assign different bands to specific districts. As you can imagine, the only way they could assess the needs of a particular household was actually to visit it. Perhaps they took prayer requests or did health surveys, whatever was necessary to determine the situation. Then they took the information back to the band, and, depending on what was required, a member of the band went to address the need. In essence, that band would adopt that family. Can't focus on a Bible study because of a leaky faucet? No problem. Send in Joe the plumber. Car keeps breaking down and can't drive to Bible study or church? No problem. Send in Mike the mechanic. Can't focus because of being a single mom with four young kids and a messy house? Send in a missionary mother who will help to set the house in order and assist in training the children. What a powerful impact we could make in our communities through such a program.

Many out there haven't been reached with the gospel simply because of the mistakes they made early in life with drugs, teen pregnancy, alcohol, etc. They desire a new life, but the vicissitudes of their present existence just hinder their every effort. Single mothers may not have a clue about keeping their house or training their children. Through corporate evangelism we can help them and relieve their suffering, demonstrating the love of Christ. Such work is the gospel with flesh on it.

Unfortunately, the great momentum gained during this period of corporate evangelism through the Christian Helpers Bands was lost, at least in part, because of the issues between our denomination and the leader of the program in Chicago, J. H. Kellogg. However, it wasn't Kellogg's method or blueprint to start with. Again, the idea of having a band of Christians with a diversity of gifts has its origin in heaven, a fact evidenced by the fact that it resurfaced in a major way during the 1920s.

One of the more noted Seventh-day Adventist medical evangelists, who picked up the corporate evangelism baton and did an amazing work, was John H. N. Tindall. Tindall was a man of professional experience and many talents. While he ws at Loma Linda University Dr. Calvin Thrash, cofounder of Uchee Pines Institute, wrote, in a research paper, of John Tindall's faith and work:

"John H. N. Tindall was undoubtedly prepared by the Holy Spirit prior to his conversion for the work that he was later to do. Endowed by nature with a strong and outgoing personality, he had had experience in newspaper work, in legal training, and was also a promoter of various enterprises in his early years" ("John H. N. Tindall: Fifty Years a Gospel-Medical Missionary Evangelist," [research paper, Loma Linda University, April 1969]).

In 1910 Ellen G. White had a vision that became known as the "medical evangelism vision." Afterward she described how the Lord had shown her a change in the method to reach the cities:

"During the night of February 27 [1910], a representation was given me in which the unworked cities were presented before me as a living reality, and I was plainly instructed that there should be a decided change from past methods of working. For months the situation has been impressed on my mind, and I urge that companies be organized and diligently trained to labor in our important cities. These workers should labor two and two, and from time to time all should meet together to relate their experiences, to pray and to plan how to reach the people quickly, and thus, if possible, redeem the time" (manuscript 21, 1910).

Her pleas did not go unheeded. John Burden, the College of Medical Evangelists (now Loma Linda University Medical Center) business manager, and others asked Tindall to put together a team of medical evangelists or medical missionaries and test God's method there in southern California.

John H. N. Tindall had trained at Loma Linda in several areas, including dietetics, physical therapy, and chemistry. He believed that his understanding of the human body and nutrition would bolster his evangelistic efforts. He was correct. Several of our churches today in Oklahoma and Texas exist because of the methods he utilized and that he first tested in San Bernardino, California. One health-oriented series resulted in 100 baptisms, $18,000 raised, and $10,500 in pledges made for the building of a new church (Thrash, p. 5).

Another series in Indiana had a Bible instructor and a medical assistant, both paid by the local conference. Nineteen other volunteers rounded out the staff. They included a "businessman, a singer, and six nurses, all of whom were able to contribute to the support of the company." The evangelistic campaign ended with the baptism of 60 and the purchase of a church building. The local mayor, a rabbi, and a number of businessmen paid for it. This is the perfect demonstration of how company, or corporate, evangelism works in general and in laboring for the rich specifically. By ministering to the health needs of the wealthy, it led to a church that would open the way to help the poorer classes (*ibid.*, p. 4).

Tindall presented health lectures to police and fire departments, showing the relationship between diet and food combinations to a person's reaction time. As you can imagine, the officers and firefighters found it interesting. John Tindall took very seriously a statement by Ellen White: "There are some who think that the question of diet is not of sufficient importance to be included in their evangelistic work. But such make a great mistake" (*Testimonies for the Church*, vol. 9, p. 112).

The methods that Tindall employed could reach people of all classes. In May of 1926 he spoke to an audience of 400 businesspeople. How did he get them all interested in coming to a meeting? The answer is health evangelism. It worked then, and it will do so again.

Through such an approach Tindall believed that he was able to reach a class of people that he could never have done as a Seventh-day Adventist minister alone. Now, isn't that the method of Christ?

CHAPTER 9

BEEHIVE PARTNERSHIPS

With so many irons in the fire, how can a church or ministry keep up with a Beehive project? One church or Beehive organization cannot shoulder all of its many facets. There should be partnerships that include churches, businesses, individuals, and independent, like-minded ministries.

We see a wonderful example in 2 Chronicles 17 that took place during the reign of King Jehoshaphat. Notice that "the Lord was with Jehoshaphat" (verse 3) and that the ruler "sought to the Lord God of his father, and walked in his commandments, and not after the doings of Israel" (verse 4). As a result, "the Lord stablished the kingdom in his hand" (verse 5). "And his heart was lifted up in the ways of the Lord: moreover he took away the high places and groves out of Judah" (verse 6).

First of all, we see that God was with Jehoshaphat. Second, the Lord was with him because he "sought to the Lord" and "walked in his commandments" and did not do that which was popular. In other words, as it was then, so it is now: it was not popular to live according to God's commandments, even among His people. Nor is it popular to seek the Lord for answers. But the Bible says that if anyone lacks wisdom, they should ask the Lord (James 1:5) for His eternal principles. Jehoshaphat sought the Lord, and what happened? The Lord showed him great favor, establishing the kingdom under Jehoshaphat's leadership. Then something truly amazing happened. In 2 Chronicles 17:6, it says that the king's heart was lifted up in the "ways of the Lord." It meant that Jehoshaphat had a mind and heart to do what God wanted him to do. Notice that as he fixed on God's will, the first thing he did was to begin a process of revival and reformation. He removed the idolatry from within the church. Then his next move was absolutely incredible.

"Also in the third year of his reign he sent his princes, even Ben-hail, and Obadiah, and Zechariah, and Nethanel, and Micaiah, to teach in the cities of Judah; and with them the Levites, even Shemaiah, and Nethaniah, and Zebadiah, and Asahel, and Shemiramoth, and Jehonathan, and Adonijah, and Tobijah, and Tob-adonijah, the Levites; and with them Elishama and Jehoram, the priests. And they taught in Judah, having the book of the law of Jehovah with them; and they went about throughout all the cities of Judah, and taught among the people. And the fear of Jehovah fell upon all the kingdoms of the lands that were round about Judah, so that they made no war against Jehoshaphat. And some of the Philistines brought Jehoshaphat presents, and silver for tribute; the Arabians also brought him flocks, seven thousand and seven hundred rams, and seven thousand and seven hundred he-goats.

And Jehoshaphat waxed great exceedingly; and he built in Judah castles and cities of store. And he had many works in the cities of Judah; and men of war, mighty men of valor, in Jerusalem" (verses 7-13, ASV).

Here we find several things:

1. Revival began with putting away idolatry (verse 6).
2. Revival and reformation must go together.
3. Therefore the king dispatched officials or "princes" or leaders (verse 7).
4. Having the book of the law of Jehovah, they taught in the cities (verse 7).
5. The Levites joined them in teaching the Word in the cities (verse 8).
6. The priests also joined them in teaching the Word in the cities (verse 8).
7. As a result of the teaching, the fear of God fell on all kingdoms and lands (verse 10).
8. The Gentiles came to the king (verse 11).
9. The king set up many projects (integrated evangelism) in the city (verses 12 and 13).

What does this historical account of Jehoshaphat during the time of the kings of Judah say to us today? We believe a great deal of it is germane to the very mission of the Beehive and its drive to promote unity and partnerships for the final work of God. You see, Jesus, the King of kings, is sending leaders of every variety, i.e., businesspeople, professionals, and students, who are laypeople, and they will be joined by religious leaders, both on the local and conference levels, and teach the Word of God in the cities. As stressed throughout this manual, this final push is relational and needs to go where people are (in the cities) to mingle with them, sympathize with them, and minister to their needs.

If you look closely, you will see echoes of the first and second angel's messages of the book of Revelation from 2 Chronicles. Revelation 14:6 and 7 declare that the everlasting gospel will go with a loud voice to every nation, kindred, tongue, and people. Second Chronicles 17:11 states that the Arabians and the Philistines (Gentiles) brought their gifts to the king. Why? Well, the answer is in verse 10: "And the fear of the Lord fell upon all the kingdoms of the land." Proverbs 9:10 declares that "the fear of the Lord is the beginning of wisdom: and the knowledge of the Holy is understanding." If the fear of the Lord is associated with the beginning of wisdom, then we see that the people of that day began to receive—from those partnerships going into the cities—knowledge of God. Remembering the first angel's message of Revelation 14:7 to "fear God, and give glory to him" is also a message of "making God known" to the world in these last days. Do you see the end-time parallel?

What happened as a result of the Gentiles bringing gifts to the king? The Bible says in 2 Chronicles 17:12 that the king "waxed great exceedingly," which resulted in much of the king's work being in the cities. But why point out this in a section dedicated to expounding upon Beehive partnerships and networking? Well, Jesus said in John 17:21 that His desire was that His disciples would be one. The king in 2 Chronicles 17 has involved leaders (princes, officials, merchants). Unlike the Levites, who are born into the religious order of the priesthood, and the priests, who officiated in the Temple, they were laypeople. But he sent them to be joined by Levites (by the way, the word "Levite" means "joined") and priests. The king formed a partnership (as we would phrase it today) to unite laypeople with pastors and conference officials to bring the Word of God to the cities. To produce genuine revival and reformation, God needs His representatives to partner for the final push as we give the final warning before Jesus comes.

Church Partnerships. The Beehive must form partnerships with local churches. It is important to the Beehive concept that it works within the overall mission of the church. Put simply, the Beehive should essentially be the connective tissue that extends the church's reach beyond its walls. That may involve self-supporting ministries, businesses, or small groups of various types. The goal is to get out of the church building and build up the kingdom of Christ.

Many churches struggle with how to be relevant in our postmodern world. They import methods from the world to try to entertain people into the church. But such things are not, have not been, and never will be God's way. In addition, many church members are living out their Christian experience as the "frozen chosen" or "pew warmers" who are simply apathetic and indifferent, relying on the pastor or someone else to do what they should be engaged in.

For congregations with these specific problems, as well as those that are evangelistically minded but just don't have any idea of how to get the church mobilized, this Beehive blueprint provides innovative ways to bring your church back to where it will be a functioning center of spiritual activity for the community. Any church can become a Beehive partner and build a network of channels to advance God's cause in its area.

Self-supporting Ministry Partnerships. We encourage self-supporting ministries who are doing a great individual work to continue their divinely appointed mission, but to expand their reach through a Beehive partnership.

Surprisingly, you can often find several self-supporting ministries doing the same thing in the same area, but struggling to stay afloat financially. Here is where the Beehive partnership can help to sustain them in many ways.

First, the Beehive should be the connection between ministries with the same zeal and vision that could cooperate to accomplish the same goals. Christ said that often the children of the world are wiser than the children of God. That is certainly true today as we see Taco Bell restaurants partnering with KFC to reduce overhead by sharing smaller buildings. In spirit, ministries can do the same thing to remain sustainable. Second, the Beehive International, Inc. (this ministry), is available to conduct weekend workshops to show other ministries how to create entrepreneurial opportunities that can help to support the ministry financially.

The Beehive welcomes all self-supporting organizations to contact us to hear some of the exciting ideas we have for networking and finishing God's work.

Partnerships With Existing Businesses. When we formed The Beehive International, we asked ourselves a critical question: Will our businesses and those of God's people ever be worth more in the future than they are at this moment in earth's history, and are they aligned closely with the last challenge of warning and winning the millions of people on earth? We encourage you to ask this of your business.

Those businesses that want to use their services in the furtherance of God's work should consider partnerships as we look to reach the cities. We recognize that many businesses and the men and women who run them desire to do a greater work for the Lord. However, many times the problem of securing the bottom line or maintaining a professional practice makes it difficult to serve. It is through a Beehive partnership that a business can get involved in several ways:

1. A Beehive business partner can plug into God's work and make a difference in their city by volunteering goods and services. Often many of God's people don't realize the need to have basic business skills to run an organization. Here is where an existing business can help by conducting workshops at local churches covering such topics as accounting/bookkeeping, marketing, social networking, computer skills, etc.

2. When time is a challenge for a local business (and it usually is), that business can become a partner and supporter by becoming a "Beehive Business," contributing tax-deductible dollars to finance local city projects and outreach efforts.

The Beehive can be a source for encouragement and activity in every major city. The time has come to turn every situation and opportunity into one that is proactively growing the kingdom of God and, as a result, "they all may be one; even as thou, Father, art in me, and I in thee, that they also may be one in us: that the world may believe that thou hast sent me" (John 17:21).

APPENDIX

THE BEEHIVE ORGANIZATION

The Beehive International, Inc., is a nonprofit 501(c) 3 organization set up to provide educational and humanitarian relief throughout the world. Like all nonprofits, a board of directors governs The Beehive. The Lord has led this ministry providentially, providing The Beehive with the best and brightest. Serving on our board are business leaders with more than 40 years of entrepreneurial experience; several authors, one of whom is a professor; an international restaurant and bakery executive; a veteran media executive; and a human resources expert. The staff members of this rapidly growing ministry are all members in good standing in the Seventh-day Adventist Church.

The Beehive is located in multiple locations around the world. We have offices in Atlanta, Georgia; Phoenix, Arizona; and Port-au-Prince, Haiti. The parent organization, however, has within its structure several arms set up for both service and to fuel the Beehive's various ministries financially.

Our Promise to God

This Beehive Ministry prayer to God is always that He will keep us faithful. We have vowed to follow the exact details of the instructions that God has shown us. In the late 1800s God had men and women around the world that were working tirelessly along integrated evangelism lines to accomplish the great last mission on earth. Sadly, though, there arose contentions and divisions in the church. Despite clear instructions to remain united, they did not, and it has had deep, lasting effects.

We hope to remain faithful in brotherly love to see laity and clergy work harmoniously as a united front, once and for all, to accomplish what was started many years ago.

Our hope is that many will unite and adopt this method so that we may lead millions to Christ and then go home to be with Him. After 170 years it is time now more than ever that God's people unite to finish the work entrusted to us. The opportunity has come for the many separate existing ministries who are doing great things for God to work together and grab hold of Christ's methods, which alone yield true success.

We believe that God Himself has resurrected the Beehive method of integrated personal evangelism to accomplish His final work. Not only is it effective in bringing people to Christ—it also builds character in the process. By taking our directions from Him through the Bible and the writings of Ellen White, we have the very principles to succeed if we faithfully carry those divine instructions out. By His leading and by His Spirit, in a united manner, we will do all that is needed. We invite you to catch the vision and join us as we step out in extreme faith.

We also invite you to learn more about our health program, The New Life Challenge:

The New Life Challenge is a 10-week health program that came about as a result of the idea that through a healthier lifestyle, anyone could dramatically enrich their overall mental, physical, and social well-being. It is based on spiritual principles surrounding the historical and biblical character Daniel. It has gone around the world and is widely known as a Christ-centered health evangelism training for churches, an outreach tool on secular college campuses, and an array of health seminars for secular and religious audiences.

The Beehive has partnered with several organizations, including Loma Linda University, to bring relief as well as agricultural development to the country of Haiti. Through our partnership the Beehive International is setting up an agricultural school that will assist in helping the people in Haiti to become self-sustaining. The farm will also serve a location from which to work the city of Port-au-Prince.

For more information about our mission work, city mission workshops, or health trainings, you can write, e-mail, or call The Beehive using the information below:

Telephone: 1-866-816-1844

Or contact us via our Web site at

BeehiveVision.com